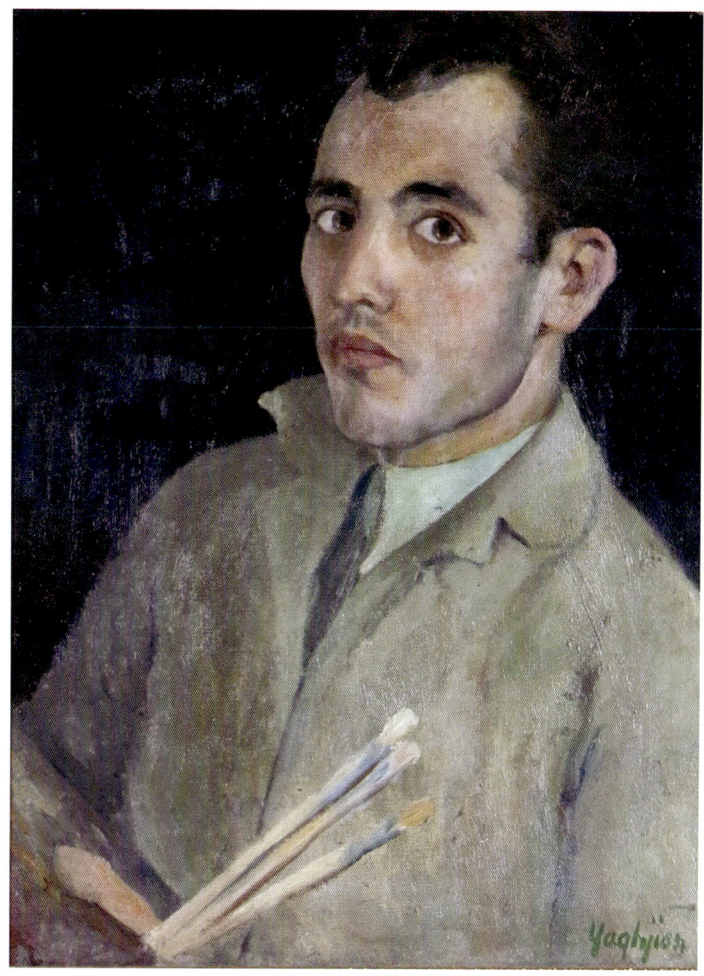

Self Portrait, 1931 • Oil on board • 24 x 18

Edmund Yaghjian

A Retrospective

South Carolina State Museum

March 16 - September 16, 2007

Published in conjunction with the exhibition "Edmund Yaghjian: A Retrospective" at the South Carolina State Museum in the Lipscomb Gallery March 16-September 16, 2007.

Exhibition curators: Paul Matheny, Chief Curator of Art, SC State Museum and Sharon Campbell, Independent Curator and Appraiser.

Catalog essays: Sharon Campbell, Paul Matheny and Robin Waites, Excecutive Director, Historic Columbia Foundation.

Color plates and Flynn Hall photograph by Jeff Salter with the exception of plates from lending institutions which have provided their own images.

Catalog design: Majken Blackwell

South Carolina State Museum
301 Gervais Street
P.O. Box 100107
Columbia, SC 29202
803.898.4921
www.southcarolinastatemuseum.org

Printed in Canada

Contents

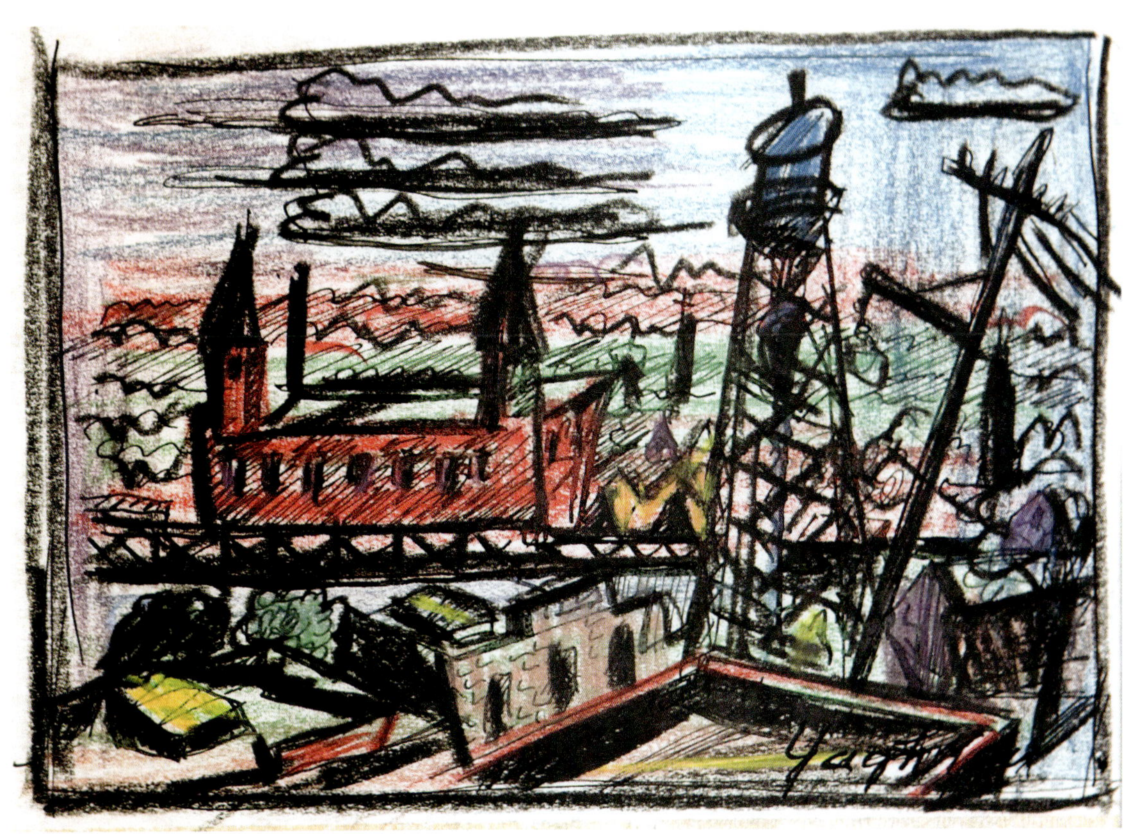

Olympia Water Tower, c. 1950 • Pencil and crayon on paper • 5 x 7 • South Carolina State Museum

Foreword

The South Carolina State Museum is honored to present this retrospective exhibition focusing on the career and life of one of South Carolina's most important visual artists and art educators, Edmund Yaghjian. His influence continues to be evident across the Palmetto State by way of his leadership as the first chairman of the Department of Art at the University of South Carolina, through the many distinguished South Carolina artists he trained and inspired, and visually through his paintings.

This project has proven to be one of the most involved art exhibitions for an individual artist that the South Carolina State Museum has hosted. This exhibition will captivate the public with Yaghjian's very early and rarely-viewed paintings of New York City from the early 1930s, his more familiar scenes of Columbia from the mid-1940s on, and all of the places that he lived and visited in between, including Missouri and Vermont.

The South Carolina State Museum is committed to producing exhibitions of excellence, and this retrospective directly reflects our philosophy. Our goal and mission is to provide a unique, educational and captivating experience for the people of our state and their visitors. We look forward to fulfilling this objective with future exhibitions of South Carolina's talented artists.

William Calloway
Executive Director, South Carolina State Museum

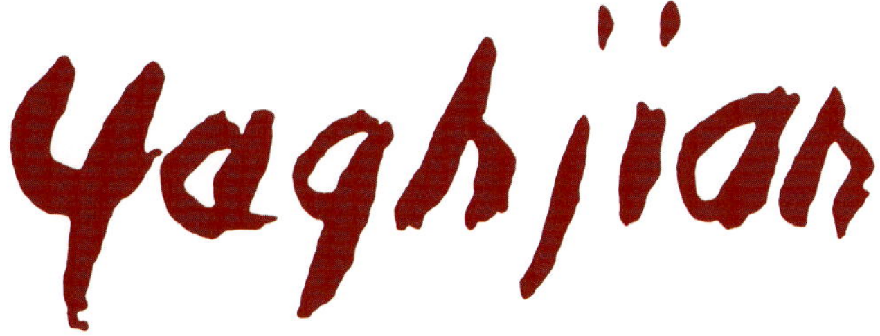

Edmund Yaghjian

Armenian-American, 1905 -1997

1905 - 1945

Believing that artists should lead by example, Edmund Yaghjian spent the first half of his life as a member of existing social and artistic communities, then devoted himself wholeheartedly to helping create them in South Carolina. Yaghjian's life was built around communities, from his birthplace in Armenia to his childhood home in an Armenian-American neighborhood to that of the art schools he attended, to artists' communities in New York and Columbia, South Carolina. His belief in a nurturing camaraderie and the fostering of creativity was the foundation of his life - artistic, familial, and educational.

With tensions increasing between Armenians and Turks living in Armenia and with hope for a better future, Samuel Yaghjian immigrated to America and made plans for his wife, Sultan, and his two young sons, Kagharshag and Keriken, to follow as soon as possible. In 1907 they joined him in the immigrant community of Providence, Rhode Island. There were many similar close-knit Armenian-American communities across the country, and the Yaghjian family chose Providence partly by virtue of its promising name. Samuel Yaghjian was an entrepreneur who opened a tobacconist shop that soon grew into a busy grocery store, a family business that the Yaghjian children were expected to take over and continue. When Keriken entered public school with its more diverse community of students, his family felt his name should be Anglicized, thus he became Edmund (Waites, R. 1996).

Edmund Yaghjian's life in Providence was filled with activity. During his school years he worked for a tailor, acted and ushered in amateur theatrical productions, and sold newspapers. On Saturdays he took classes at the Rhode Island School of Design (RISD). In 1922, after graduating from high school, Edmund began working full-time in the family grocery store. Drawing portraits was one of his passions; he drew at home and on brown paper grocery bags at work. He remained at the grocery until one of the ministers of the church where Edmund taught Sunday school noticed his ability in portraiture and convinced a wealthy parishioner to give him a scholarship to RISD (Waites, R. 1996). This scholarship is one of the pivotal points in the artist's life; without the scholarship and its accompanying vote of confidence, though a talented artist, Yaghjian might have remained a grocer.

Three years later, the young artist had completed the four-year BFA program at RISD, graduated with honors and turned down an offer from the school to teach. Yaghjian was determined to live in New York, and study at the Art Students League (ASL), a venture spawned possibly at the urging of his teacher, former ASL student John Robertson Frazier. Yaghjian was a student at the ASL, arguably the best art school in the country at the time, from 1930 to 1933. He studied with Stuart Davis; figure painter and portraitist, Ivan Olinsky; and painter William Von Schlegell, who introduced his students to the work of Gauguin and Van Gogh. These influences, along with Yaghjian's own interest in the vibrant paintings by El Greco, seem to have germinated for years, becoming more evident in the 1950s.

From its inception in 1875, ASL students elected the administration and chose their teachers. The curriculum was very broad and, even today, does not favor any one particular style of painting. Because of this inclusiveness and vitality, the history of the League reflects the important events in the artistic growth of America. Among the League's first teachers were William Merritt Chase, J. Alden Weir, and Robert Henri. Among those in the 1920s and 30s were John Sloan, Stuart Davis, Thomas Hart Benton, John Steuart Curry, George Grosz, Max Weber, and Hans Hofmann. There appears to have been a strong sense of artistic community at that time involving faculty and students from the ASL, National Academy of Design, artists' unions and societies as well as community art centers such as those established in Harlem by the African-American artist, Augusta Savage. This was true even though the structure and goals of the organizations were dissimilar.

Though most American artists in the 1800s had been trained at least partly in Europe, by the early 20th century, art in the United States was far less European. In 1887 Henry James said, "It sounds like a paradox, but it is a very simple truth, that when today we look for 'American art' we find it mainly in Paris. When we find it out of Paris, we at least find a great deal of Paris in it" (Adler, K., Hirschler, E., & Weinberg, B., 2006). At least as early as Robert Henri's 1915 - 1928 tenure at the ASL there was an interest in developing an art based on an individual reaction to the American environment, in part a response to the ideal of the immigrant becoming American. In the early years of the twentieth century this search for a truly American art gave the ASL an impetus to hire Thomas Hart Benton, John Steuart Curry, and John Sloan, artists whose bodies of work were about the various aesthetic souls of America.

In addition to such American influences as the Ash Can School, Regionalists, and artists from the Harlem Renaissance, some of whom studied at the ASL, there were threads of earlier European influences from artists who studied in Europe. For instance, William Merritt Chase studied at the Royal Academy in Munich, and his École des Beaux-Arts-trained counterpart, J. Alden Weir, both taught at the League beginning in the 1870s. The expatriate artists who lived and worked in Paris and London in the late 1800s returned to America and influenced artists in Philadelphia, Boston, and New York. As Dorothy Grafly commented in *Art Digest*, about the 1938 exhibition at the Pennsylvania Academy of the Fine Arts, "Absent entirely is the flood of French imitations,...that scarcely 10 years ago dominated American painting exhibitions" (Stamm, G. 1972). This exhibition included New York works by Yaghjian in addition to those by Raphael Soyer, Stuart Davis and Guy Péne du Bois. In Philadelphia, home of many of the expatriate artists from the 1800s, this was perhaps a surprising comment. Clearly, by this time, however, art in America was largely identified with subjects drawn from the American scene, rendered frequently in understandable representational styles. Views of the countryside and the city, especially New York, had become subjects of increasing interest among artists. During the 1910s and 1920s, artists saw the city as vibrant, powerful, growing, teeming with activity, and, in particular, it was about the future. Though in some quarters this remained the case, during the 1930s many artists took the economic times to heart and turned their attention not to the sky-piercing buildings overhead but to the social concerns on the ground.

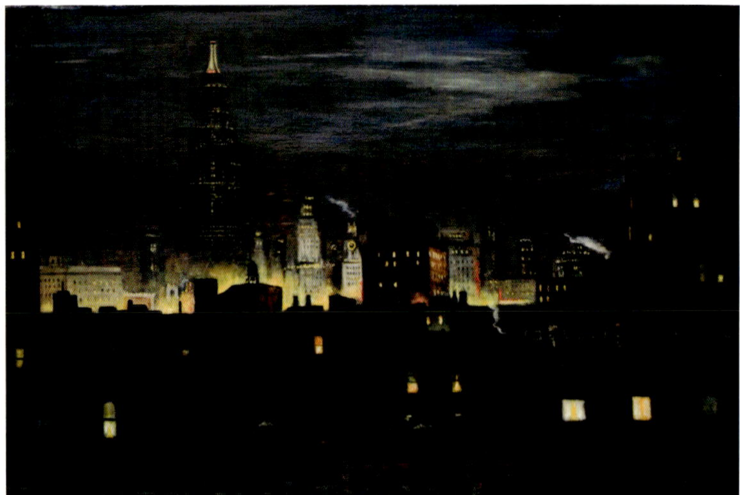

Night in Manhattan, 1936

Artists came to New York from such diverse locations as Russia, Missouri, Armenia, Oklahoma, Paris, Munich, Kansas City, Rhode Island, Poland, and Cape Cod. Led as always by student interest, the ASL hired Hans Hofmann, George Grosz, and Jan Matulka, among others, and through them the League received a strong infusion of modernism to match the interest in realism and American subject matter. So, though Yaghjian "dreamt of going to Europe to paint, (he) settled for New York instead" (Stamm, G. 1972). In New York he had access to the art and the breadth of ideas from both Europe and America. In fact, when John Sloan became president of the League in 1931, he ascribed its success to its furnishing "such a varied menu of nourishment for the hungry art student, ranking from the conservative to the ultra-modern" (Pisano, R., 1987).

Looking back on Yaghjian's move to New York, 1930 was not an auspicious time to begin a career as an artist. The Library of Congress described the situation this way in *Life of the People*:

One of the Depression's first casualties was the art market. ...Growing frustration and despair led many of (the artists) to a new-found identification with other victims of the economic crisis. An art of social content and wide accessibility gained favor, as artists sought...a mass, democratized market.

The result was an art in which urban, rural, and industrial scenes were all part of the great connection among people of all situations -- those who worked in offices, on the land, in factories, and those who could find no work at all.

Despite the economy, 1930 was the moment Edmund Yaghjian chose to come to New York. A year later his work, primarily portraits, was listed by the League's year-end report as "best of the year." In New York his interest and inspiration were increasingly focused on the urban environment

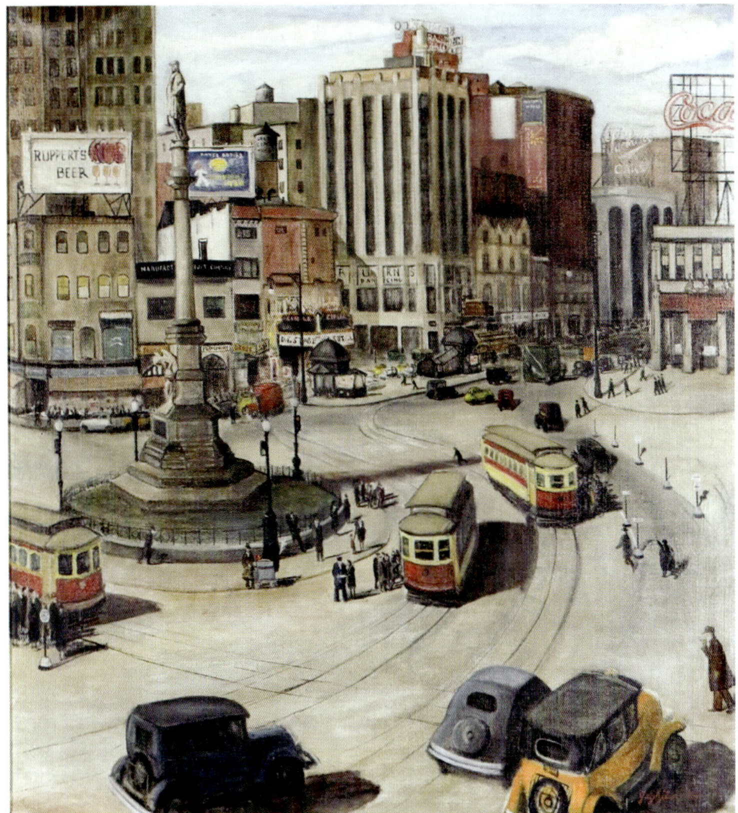

Columbus Circle, 1934

and his portraits represented in the 1932 exhibitions at the "Society of Independent Artists Annual Exhibition" and the "American Art Association Exhibition" were among his last. He arrived in the city a portrait painter and departed in the 1940s an American urban scene painter. His large vigorous canvases painted in New York focused on the power and excitement of the nourishing, forceful city. He created energetic, often aerial views of Times Square, Columbus Circle, the East River, the Harlem River, Central Park, and Broadway, and scenes of tugboats and industry, all filled with the city's own life. Unlike some of his colleagues, among them Raphael Soyer, Reginald Marsh and Isabel Bishop, he did not paint interiors or street scenes showing individuals or small groups of people. His people are seen as part of the city, amorphous masses along with the steam from buildings, traffic, and smoke rising from the stacks of the tugboats.

In 1932 Yaghjian curated an exhibition of works by artists from the League for Vose Galleries, then in Providence, Rhode Island. The catalog foreword was written by John Sloan:

There can be no doubt that if there is now, or is to be, among us an art that can be called American, a very great part of its evidence must be looked for among the works of what are called the younger and 'unknown' artists. That an artist is unknown is no crime of his commission, it is much more likely to be a crime of omission of the part of the art conscious public (if there be any such)....they are independents, they are young, and they are ready to be known.

Among the artists chosen by Yaghjian for this exhibition were Burgoyne Diller, already a champion of abstract, geometric-based art; John W. Gregory, one of Sloan's students who later became a well-known photographer; Charles Trumbo Henry, who often painted the industrial aspects of small towns; and John Tazewell Robertson, a student of Sloan, Benton, and Curry at the Art Students League and, surprisingly enough, of Louis Comfort Tiffany, at the Tiffany Foundation. Clearly, Yaghjian had broad interests and an open mind. Among his colleagues were modernists, abstract artists, regionalists, social realists, and urban regionalists.

As part of a group of artists considered by many to be the next group of rising stars, Yaghjian tried to make a living selling his artwork. The first exhibition of his New York scenes was held in 1933 at the Hotel Brevoort. Next, a 1934 painting, *Columbus Circle*, was shown at the Providence Art Club and at the Pennsylvania Academy. He was represented in the 1936 International Exhibition at the Carnegie Institute and at the Third Biennial Exhibition of Contemporary American Painting at the Whitney Museum. That same year marked the 60th anniversary of the Art Students League, and his painting, *East River*, was shown along with works by Reginald Marsh, Isabel Bishop, and others at the League. He was included in the 1938 Pennsylvania Academy of the Fine Arts annual exhibition with Raphael Soyer, Stuart Davis and Guy Péne du Bois, and one of his major works, *Night in Manhattan*, was in the 1939 New York World's Fair. In 1940, "Nocturnal New York", his first solo exhibition at a commercial gallery, was at Kraushaar, where his work had been in group exhibitions with Sloan, Luks, Glackens, Prendergast, and Péne du Bois. Kraushaar was among the most influential galleries in the city and was very selective in its choice of artists.

In addition to the ASL and the city itself, there were other influences on Yaghjian. Joseph Delaney, an African-American artist and younger brother of the better-known artist, Beauford Delaney, also enrolled at the League in 1930. While there, Delaney was a student of Thomas Hart Benton, who inspired him to document the life of African-Americans. Delaney went on to teach at the Harlem and Brooklyn settlement houses and later at the League. Other influential black artists with ties to Harlem and the New York artistic community were Romare Bearden and Jacob Lawrence. Bearden studied with George Grosz at the League in 1936 and was a friend of Stuart Davis, one of Yaghjian's primary mentors. Lawrence, whose narrative paintings, *The Migration Series*, depicted the move of African-Americans from the rural South to the great Northern cities after World War I, was a very influential artist and teacher. *The Migration Series* was created in 1940-41 and exhibited at the Downtown Gallery, marking the first time works by an African-American artist were shown at a commercial New York gallery. Coincidentally, the Downtown Gallery showed works by Stuart Davis, John Marin, Ben Shahn, and precisionist painters Charles Sheeler and Edmund Lewandowski. It appears that Stuart Davis and the Downtown Gallery were pivotal influences in the interaction among New York modernists, Harlem-based artists, and artists associated with the ASL. These influences from African-American artists became more visible in Yaghjian's later series of works related to Ossining, New York; Wallingford, Vermont; and, in particular, to South Carolina.

Other major forces at work in the 1930s and 40s were the looming threat from Germany, which increased immigration from Europe to America, the Works Progress Administration's Federal Art Project (WPA FAP), a Federal initiative for artists in response to the Depression, and World War II. Yaghjian and most of his friends and colleagues were part of the WPA's FAP. This program put over 3500 artists to work creating over 15,000 works of art. Yaghjian's *The White Church* was created in 1936, as part of that program. Financial conditions remained precarious for the artist. When World War II began, Yaghjian, who had stomach ulcers, had no duty in the war effort and remained in New York successfully teaching and painting. His work was represented in the 1944 Metropolitan Museum of Art's exhibition "Portrait of America." Though there were positive reviews and a great deal of interest in the paintings, sales of his work over the course of the late 1930s and the 1940s were not enough to live on.

While a member of the elected administration of the Art Students League, Yaghjian had also begun to teach. First, he held private lessons at the Men's Residence Club where he lived. Then, one of his first official teaching jobs began in 1934 at Great Neck Preparatory School in Long Island, New York. He remained there for several years, leaving to teach at Edgewood Park Junior College in Ossining, New York, where he was on the faculty from 1941-43. His paintings in Ossining reflect the charm and contentment of small-town life. The watercolors of train cars and small businesses foreshadow his later interest in similar subjects in South Carolina.

Yaghjian cared deeply about the role of art in society and the intellectual underpinnings of this role. He believed that artists should paint those things they know and convey these feelings to others. He felt that the artist was responsible to himself and that he "must be judged by what he tried to do" (Waites, R., 1996).

In the October 14, 1937 edition of *The Armenian Spectator,* writer Avedis Derounian quoted Yaghjian as saying:

Publicity? It isn't hard to get at all, if you are the type who goes after it. But I am not the type, that's all. [And] why should I? Doctors have their code of ethics. There is, too, an unwritten code among artists. I choose to practice it. An artist speaks through his work. All other means are superficial.

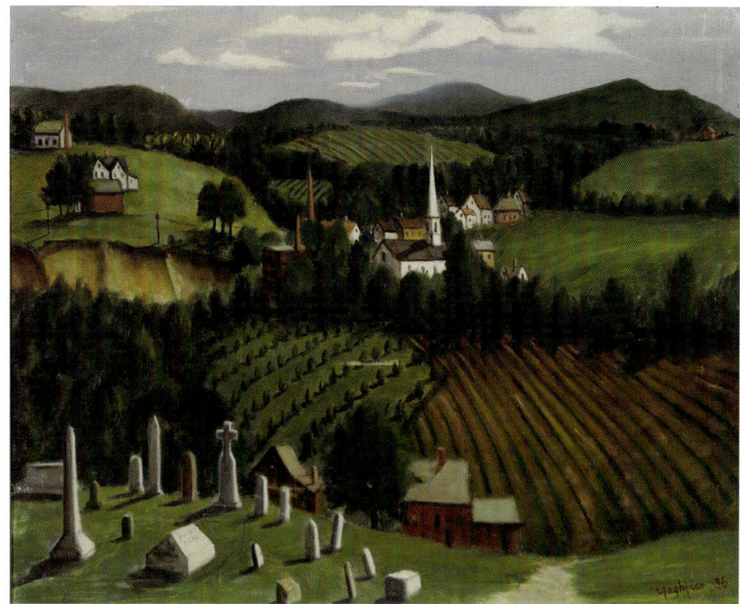

The White Church, 1936

As sales slowed in New York, Yaghjian's primary income was increasingly derived from teaching. Consequently the balance of his energy shifted toward teaching and away from painting. From 1938 to 1942, Yaghjian taught life drawing, painting, and composition at the Art Students League. As always, students at the ASL were allowed to choose their own teachers; Dorothy Candy was one of those who chose to study with Yaghjian. With her, he began a private summer school in Wilmott, New Hampshire in 1940; he began a second school the next year in West Cornwall, Connecticut, this time with Dorothy Candy, as his wife.

When Yaghjian first thought about leaving New York, he contacted his former colleagues Thomas Hart Benton and John Steuart Curry, who were chairing art departments in the Midwest. Neither department had any openings but he was offered, and accepted, a position as artist in residence at the University of Missouri, Columbia, for the academic year 1944-45. At the end of that residency he was offered a full time position at the University of South Carolina. It was a perfect turning point for him. New York had been a wonderful proving ground, he had learned from the finest teachers available, was represented by one of the best galleries in the country, and there were plans for his future with them. When he discussed the possible move to South Carolina with the Kraushaars, he was told that art in the South was dead. He knew that the move to South Carolina, or any move away from New York, would relegate him to the status of a regional painter. He took this as a challenge. In some ways, this was a perfect time for him to move to a university. After the war, the GI Bill allowed servicemen to take classes at various schools and universities, giving far more people access to education and developing American universities as a greater force in the art world.

His goals were to paint, enjoy life with his family and use his abilities to create environments which would foster creativity. Accomplished, but not innovative, his paintings were based on the life and influences of the community. By the late 1940s and early 1950s, the art world had moved toward abstraction and away from the kind of accessible, democratic works he painted.

By 1951, when Yaghjian exhibited his first southern works in Columbia, South Carolina, his palette had changed as had his style and point of view. His subject matter, now views of neighborhoods in South Carolina, was far more intimate than the earlier distant views of city buildings, streets, and harbors. Yaghjian wanted to capture rich aspects of American life before they changed or disappeared. His work consisted of modernist-inspired compositions along with a reverence and respect for the life of small cities and towns and of the people there. This is apparent in Yaghjian's watercolors of Ossining, NY; his paintings of city life in Columbia, Missouri; the quarries, landscapes, and interiors in Wallingford, Vermont; and, exuberantly, as a life's work, in Columbia, South Carolina.

Sharon Campbell, Co-curator
Edmund Yaghjian: A Retrospective

References:

Waites, Robin. (1996) *Edmund Yaghjian: Patriarch of Art in South Carolina*. Unpublished M.A. thesis, University of South Carolina.

Adler, Kathleen., Hirschler, Erica E.., & Weinberg, H. Barbara. (2006) *Americans in Paris: 1860-1900*. National Gallery, London.

Library of Congress (2000). *Art of the People: The American Scene*. Retrieved September 24, 2006 from the World Wide Web: http://www.loc.gov/exhibits/goldstein/goldamer.html

Stamm, Gunther. (1972) *Ed Yaghjian: Retrospective Exhibition*. Exhibition catalog. Columbia Museum of Art. Columbia, SC.

Pisano, Ronald. (1987) *The Art Students League: Selections from the Permanent Collection*. Exhibition catalog. Hamilton, New York. The Association.

Conversations and correspondence between the author and Patricia Phagan (Frances Lehman Loeb Art Center, Vassar College, Poughkeepsie, NY), October 30, December 21-22, 2006.

Edmund Yaghjian

1945-1997

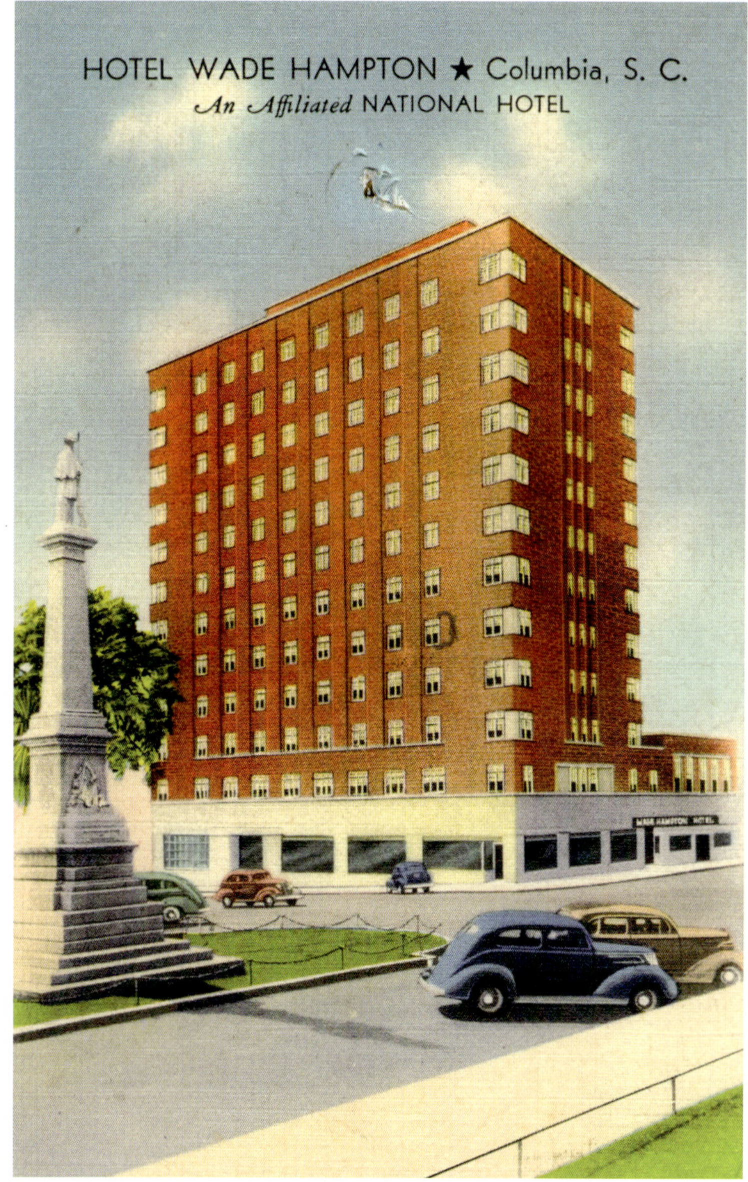

Postcard c.1940

On January 28, 1945, Edmund Yaghjian boarded a plane bound for Columbia, South Carolina. When he arrived he checked into the historic Wade Hampton Hotel on Main Street. The trip to the South was for a job interview at the University of South Carolina for the position of instructor and Chair of the Art Department. On February 2, 1945, just five days after his interview he received a letter from Norman M. Smith, President of USC, offering the young artist the position of professor and the first Chair of the Department. This began a 52 year relationship with a southern city he previously had visited for only two days.

Yaghjian arrived at the University of South Carolina on October 1, 1945. Upon entering Flynn Hall, where the art department was originally located, he was in charge of 167 students taking art classes through the department. At that time, there were 1700 students enrolled in the University (Waites, R. 1996). Yaghjian taught eighteen hours each week and focused on painting when he was not in the classroom. He served as a drawing and painting instructor at the University along with two colleagues, Augusta Wittkowsky and Ruth Morse. Yaghjian previously taught at the University of Missouri in Columbia where he held a one year teaching contract. Prior to that, he taught at the Art Students League in New York City from 1938-1942 where he was also a student and colleague of the Ashcan painters.

After leaving the cavernous land of brownstones, high rises, skyscrapers and cultural institutions of the North, Yaghjian may not have been prepared for the cultural landscape of Columbia, South Carolina. The busy New York City was much different from the places and people in South Carolina, particularly entering this society from an artist's observant perspective.

Yaghjian was warned by Antoinette Kraushaar, owner of Kraushaar Galleries where he actively exhibited and regularly sold his paintings in New York City, that the South was no place for an important artist like himself to move (Waites, R. 1996). Baltimore journalist, Henry Lewis Mencken, embellished this stereotype when he wrote in his 1920 essay, *The Sahara of the Bozart*, that the South was "almost as sterile artistically, intellectually, culturally, as the Sahara Desert - culturally about as dead as the Yucatan." In the same essay he stated, "There is not a single picture gallery worth going into, or a single orchestra capable of playing the nine symphonies of Beethoven, or a single opera-house, or a single theater devoted to a decent play."

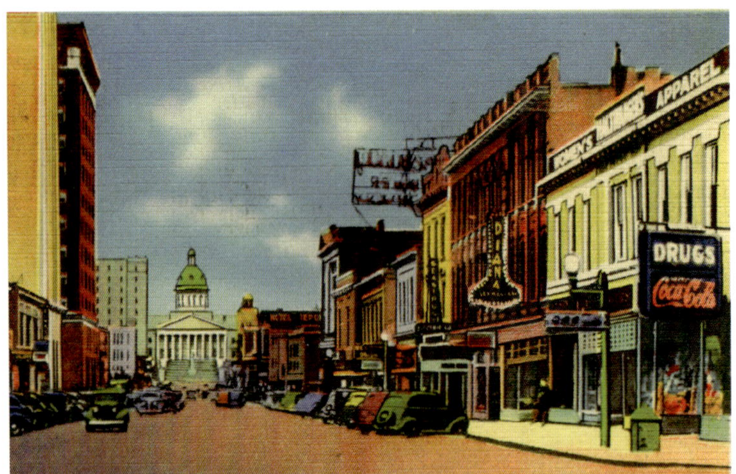

Postcard of Main Street, Columbia S.C., c. 1940

Despite the northern sentiment and Mencken's disdain for the South, the two largest cities in South Carolina had seen the beginnings of a cultural renewal just 5 years prior to his essay. The most recognized artistic renewal in this state occurred in Charleston, South Carolina, a city just over 100 miles from Columbia. Charleston had seen a cultural renewal in the form of an artistic renaissance beginning around 1915. This "Holy City" became a haven for artists influenced by the beauty, landscape and culture of the South Carolina Lowcountry including local artists Elizabeth O'Neill Verner, John Fowler Cooper, Alice Ravenel Huger Smith, Carew Rice, Anna Heyward Taylor and visiting artists including Alfred Hutty, Walker Evans, and Edward Hopper among others.

In 1915, individuals in Columbia had also begun to recognize the need for more "intellectual outlets and cultural opportunities" and by 1916 city leaders and citizens officially formed the Columbia Art Association (Lorick Library, 2006). Due to World War I, the efforts slowed and the Association collaborated with Camp Jackson, organizing lectures and other art programming for soldiers stationed at the camp. Efforts resumed for the citizens of Columbia by 1920 and the Association began to coordinate programs including lectures, concerts and exhibitions. Since there was no cultural institution in Columbia able to organize this type of programming, events occurred in individuals' homes and meeting halls in the city including the YMCA, City Council Chambers, Columbia High School, the Masonic Temple and the Town Theatre. Artists involved with these lecture programs and exhibitions were local, regional and international in scope including Clara Barrett Strait, Alice Ravenel Huger Smith, Leila Waring, Joseph Physioc, Elizabeth O'Neill Verner and Willard Hirsch, all from South Carolina; Fredrick Hibbard from Chicago, Illinois; Nison Tregor from New York and Rene Batigne from Paris, France. Some of the traveling and group exhibitions hosted by the association included a Sesqui-Centennial exhibition focusing on Columbia artists, exhibitions from the Grand Central Gallery, the American Watercolor Society and the Southern States Art League. In 1927 the city hosted "The Exhibition of Paintings by Leading Living American Artists" from Grand Central Art Galleries in New York (Craft, J. 1975). Since there was no museum or gallery to house this exhibition, individuals and hotels hosted the show in their homes and in hotel lobbies. The most ambitious exhibition from this group, "Jubilee," occurred in 1940, celebrating the 25th anniversary of the organization. It included the work of Anna Hyatt Huntington, Winslow Homer, Childe Hassam, John Singer Sargent and featured complementary exhibitions of decorative arts from the community. These included silver, glass and miniature portraits.

Unlike the Charleston Renaissance which was predominately the result of artists stimulating artistic growth in their immediate community, cultural growth in Columbia was created by individuals, business leaders and civic organizations as a way to provide art opportunities for the community. There were fewer artists living in Columbia than in Charleston during this time, and much less of an immediate revenue potential without the elevated tourist market that the S.C. Lowcountry shared with Charleston.

The South Carolina Art Education Association (SCAEA) created in 1924, began to provide a stimulus for art education in public schools in South Carolina. This Association was created as a department of the South Carolina Education Association to help increase awareness of the importance of visual arts in the state. SCAEA regularly met in Columbia and worked to encourage the community to expand arts in South Carolina within the realm of public education. According to the notes of the early conferences, they were faced with similar challenges but were making attempts for change within public schools. *The History of the South Carolina Art Education Association* (Gunter, S.F. 2002, p.5) references a 1927 Conference in Columbia where Hilda Huddle, Supervisor of Art for Columbia City Schools, proclaimed:

The aim today of the Elementary Art Course is to develop higher standards of citizenship through means of design and drawing, and an appreciation for art as

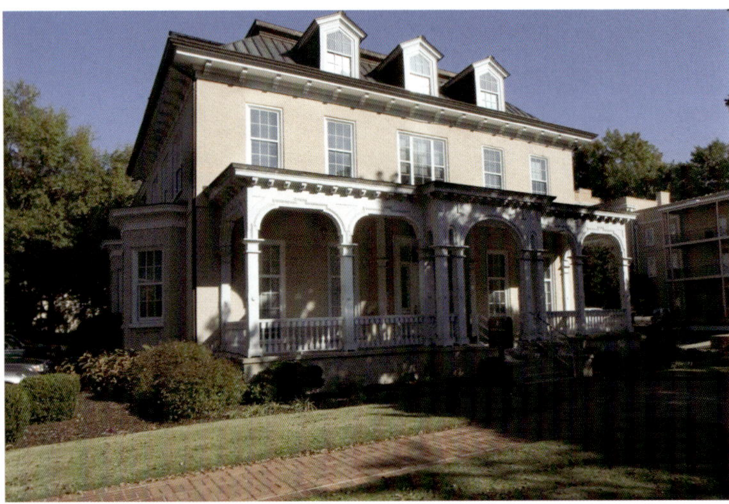
Flynn Hall, University of South Carolina

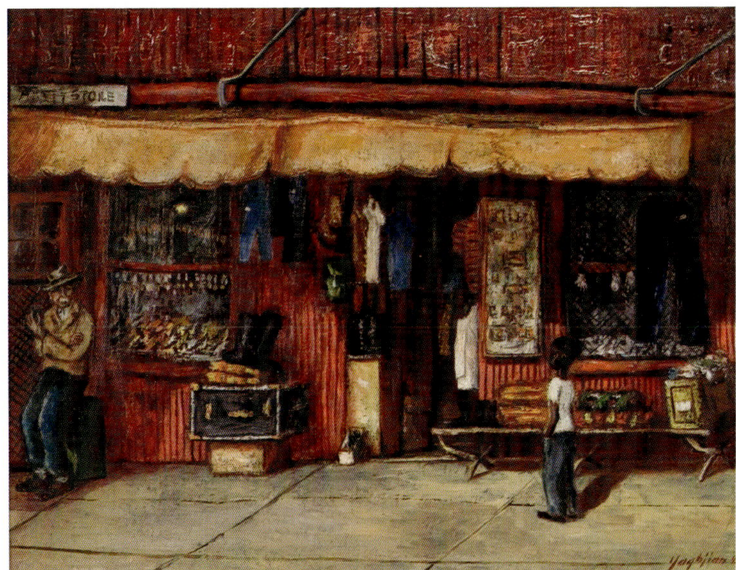

Army Store, 1946

related to life. We cannot make artists of children, not one in a thousand will ever become an actual designer, but we can give them the practical, every-day side of art that is so closely connected with the life of every individual. We no longer look upon the art course as a fad, the drawing period as the time for amusing the children, and the whole thing as intended for the talented few, but we make our course for every child in school.

This groundwork would begin to influence the first generation of artists with whom Yaghjian would come in contact when he arrived at the University of South Carolina in 1945.

By the time Yaghjian arrived in Columbia following World War II, the efforts of the Columbia Art Association seemed to have slowed other than the collaboration with Camp Jackson and the outreach with the soldiers and their families. Soon after Yaghjian's arrival in the Columbia community, he began to understand the stories from his colleagues and from his dealer, Antoinette Kraushaar. In New York City there were hundreds of commercial art galleries, numerous arts centers and museums, and a thriving art community. In Columbia, there were no museums and very little exhibition space outside the efforts of the Columbia Art Association and the University of South Carolina Department of Art. The programs organized by the Association were coordinated by upper class citizens and there was no artist based community as Yaghjian had known in New York. Despite the ongoing efforts from the citizens of Columbia that brought in exhibitions predominately focusing on artists outside of the region, there was not a core community of artists in Columbia, an important stimulus for the creative process. In an interview following his relocation, Yaghjian recalled: "I came anyway and it was dead" (Waites, R. 1996).

In 1946 Yaghjian was interviewed by Anne Searson for *The Gamecock*, the university newsletter, where he exclaimed, "We have no facilities for hanging or exhibiting paintings. With a museum would come good national and regional shows, artists beginning their careers would have an opportunity for exhibition and would not be driven from their native state to develop their talent." By 1948 Yaghjian was the Vice President of the Columbia Art Association and that same year, along with other artists from the Midlands, started the Columbia Artists Guild. His passion proved to be a positive stimulus for the Columbia arts community, which helped lead to the opening of the Columbia Museum of Art in 1950, more commercial galleries, programs and events and an obvious artist-driven community involvement with the arts that exist today.

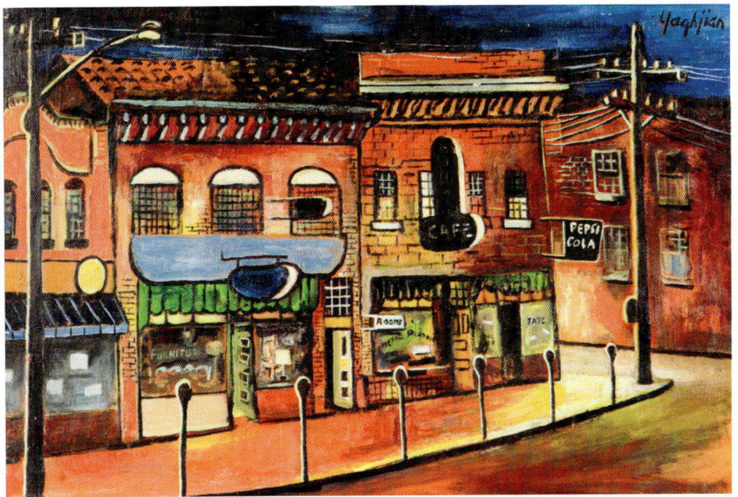

Upper Main at Night, 1970

Yaghjian continued to exhibit his work nationally even after he relocated to Columbia. Exhibitions include the Pepsi Company's Third Annual Exhibition of Paintings in 1946 at the Pennsylvania Academy of Fine Arts. Here he had also exhibited his New York paintings in 1934, 1938, and Columbia paintings again in 1949. In 1947, 1950, 1953 and 1954 he participated in the High Museum of Art's "Southeastern Annual Exhibition of Oils and Watercolors." He also participated in competitive exhibitions at the Metropolitan Museum of Art and the Birmingham Museum of Art in 1953 and 1954. In 1953 he coordinated a group exhibition at the Columbia Museum of Art with four other South Carolina artists titled "Carolina Five" that included Yaghjian, Armando del Cimmuto, William Halsey, Eugene Massin, and Gilmer Petroff. This exhibition traveled across the southeast to other museums including the Telfair Museum in Savannah, Georgia. He continued to participate in the High Museum of Art's exhibition which was turned over to the Atlanta Art Association Galleries through the end of the 1950's. In 1960 he was the focus of a one person show at the Gibbes Art Gallery titled, "Exhibition Yaghjian 1945-1960" and in 1972 the Columbia Museum of Art hosted a retrospective

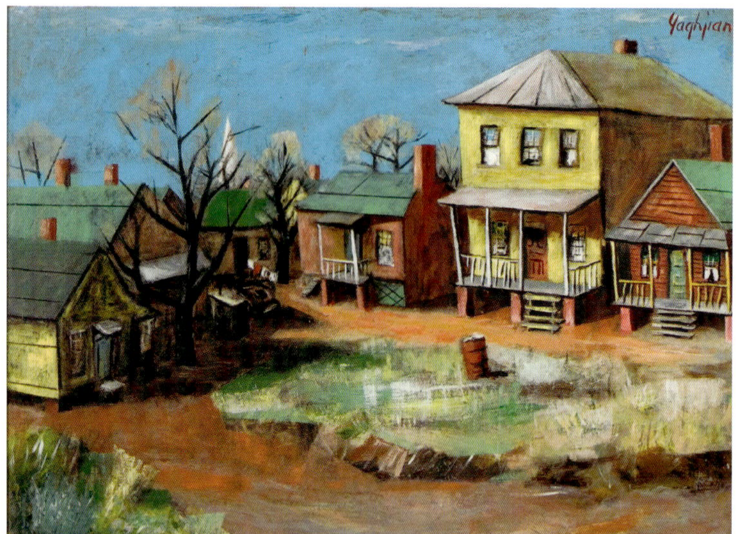

Around the Bend, circa 1950

of his work in celebration of his retirement from the University the same year (Yaghjian, E. personal papers).

While he continued to exhibit his work nationally, his subject matter quickly began to change once he settled in Columbia, reflecting the southern environment around him. Kraushaar Gallery returned all but a few of his paintings and left the opportunity open for the future if his paintings returned to subjects that embraced the northern community.

The paintings Yaghjian created after arriving in South Carolina began a lifelong search that was built on the foundations of influences he had while living in the North. He experimented with style, color and composition while focusing on familiar subject matter. He continued to embrace the ideas he gained through his association with his Art Students League colleagues, and continued to recognize the need to paint the real aspects of the immediate environment and community, painting what he knew, what was directly in front of him and embracing those truths rather than altering them for enhanced and false beautification. This eventually led him to investigate painting sites that might soon disappear, houses and buildings that were dilapidated but emulated a sense of time, stories and history that never could be replaced after they were destroyed.

The earliest Columbia, South Carolina paintings reference the realistic style that he focused on while he was in New York City and Columbia, Missouri. In 1946 his paintings reflected the commercial subjects within the main streets of the city, connecting them with his paintings and referencing his experience in New York City. These paintings present a more straight-forward nature rather than the floating bird's eye view perspective of many of the New York City scenes. The new Columbia paintings appear as snapshots of storefronts, incorporating signs and elements of the locations and give the viewer the sense of standing in front of the building, observing the activities and participating as a bystander with the picture. *Assembly Street Market* and *Army Store*, both from 1946 are two examples which exemplify this idea.

In the 1940s he began to wander into communities outside of the main streets, and embrace the beauty of textural dilapidation of shacks and shotgun houses and African-American culture outside the perimeter of the city. *Around the Bend*, circa1950, reflects the architecture and landscape to which he was drawn, particularly on Huger, Park and lower areas of Wheat Streets. One of the main thoroughfares of Columbia today, Huger Street was not as busy or even paved until the 1950s. This is illustrated most directly in his painting, *Morning on Huger Street*, circa 1955, which includes the iconic bungalow style church that still stands on Huger Street today and gas tanks that have long since been dismantled. The majority of the houses that existed on this site in 1950 are no longer there, some of which were just recently demolished. The Park Street paintings also are good representations of his love of these aesthetically and culturally rich communities. One iconographic building which he used repeatedly is Baker's Grocery, often referred to in his paintings as Park Street Grocery. This store was owned and run by Clara Baker, and was located at the corner of Park and Pendleton streets (Baker, J. personal communication). As with many of these visual documents created by Yaghjian, this building was torn down and a new structure was erected. The corner of Park and Pendleton, where Baker's Grocery once stood, is currently the location of the S.C. Department of Transportation building.

By 1950 Yaghjian had begun a series of semi-geometric flat color paintings depicting places around the city. *Corner House for Sale* from 1950, reflects what looks like a combination store front and house that is for sale in Columbia, possibly on or near Park or Wheat Street. This series of flat color paintings seems to have its roots after a trip to the artist's farm in Wallingford, Vermont, which he and his wife purchased in 1944 and spent their summers.

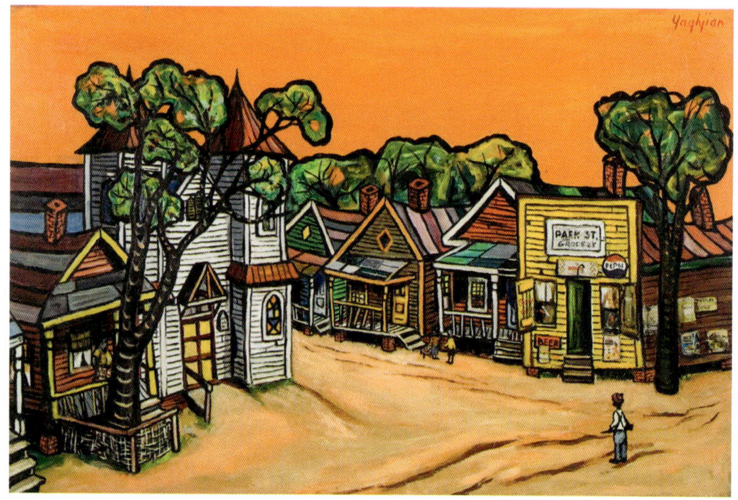

Orange Sky on Park Street, circa 1970

Two paintings, *Backstairs in Vermont* and *Kitchen in Wallingford*, are both examples of this style and dated 1949. This style was continued through the early 1950s and generated an important series of paintings depicting scenes from the South Carolina State Fair, a South Carolina swamp and what appears to be a predominantly African-American neighborhood composed of shotgun houses near an elevated train track.

Interestingly, paintings by Yaghjian of these African-American communities did not reflect his environment or the population at USC. Due to segregation, African-Americans were not admitted into the University of South Carolina until 1963. The community aesthetic of New York compared to that of the Columbia area reflects two completely different worlds. The shacks and clotheslines elevated over raked dirt yards with corroded steel 55 gallon drum trash cans in Columbia provided a completely new experience of visual culture that directly influenced and fed Yaghjian's image bank.

As an educator Yaghjian made an immediate impact in South Carolina. His passion for art education spread through his connection with the South Carolina Art Education Association and with his 1946 lecture appropriately titled, "Art is for Everyone" advocating his democratic and inclusive style of art (Gunter, S.F. 2002). The influence did not stop with the community and his desire to propagate art centers, but was a residual effect of his passion. His primary role was to teach painting and drawing at the University where he remained active from 1945-1966, and continued as the first Artist-In-Residence from 1966-1972.

Many of today's distinguished South Carolina artists were Yaghjian's students, including J. Bardin, Jak Smyrl, Jasper Johns, Sigmund Abeles, Larry Lebby, Warren Johnson (aka Blue Sky), Christian Thee, David Van Hook and Bill Buggle. Most of these students appreciated the experience in the classroom and built off of Yaghjian's foundation and developed their own unique styles separating them from their professor. One student, Jack Morris, not only followed the artistic path but also embraced the need to create museums to promote culture and industry within urban areas and helped build the current building which houses the Greenville Museum of Art in Greenville, SC.

Edmund Yaghjian continued to be a vital influence in the community after retirement, teaching lessons at the Columbia Museum of Art School, the Shepherd's Center and the Community Center at Arsenal Hill where he also regularly attended dances.

On December 2, 1997, Edmund Yaghjian passed away leaving behind an awakened public awareness of art within the community. Yaghjian's influence and impact continue to be felt today, and his stylized paintings of Columbia are important works of art, acting as documents and personally reflecting this community that was so important to him.

Paul Matheny, Chief Curator of Art
South Carolina State Museum

References:

Baker, John. Personal communication, Sep. 21, 2006.

Craft, J. (1975) *The Columbia Art Association, 1915-1975;* The Columbia Museum of Art, 1950-1975, Columbia, South Carolina: A History. Columbia Museums of Art and Science.

Gunter, S.F. (2002) *The History of the South Carolina Art Education Association: 1924- 2002.* Retrieved June 9, 2006 from the World Wide Web: http://www.scaea.org/history_04.doc..

Lorick Library History. (n.d.) Retrieved Nov. 14, 2006, from the World Wide Web: http://www.libsci.sc.edu/histories/special/colaartmuseum/lorick-library-history.html.

Searson, A. (1946). *The Gamecock*

Waites, R. (1996) *Edmund Yaghjian: Patriarch of art in South Carolina.* Unpublished masters thesis, University of South Carolina.

Yaghjian, E. (1930's-1990's) personal papers. private collection.

Crossing the Boundaries of Race and Class

Yaghjian's Huger Street

Edmund Yaghjian arrived in Columbia, South Carolina in the fall of 1945. The second World War had ended just months before and young men were arriving home to a city that had not changed significantly since the 1930s, but was about to experience extensive growth and the accompanying pains. Influenced by population increases, residential and commercial growth, political infighting and racial tensions, by the mid-1950s Columbia was on the cusp of physical and cultural upheaval that would change the landscape of the capital city.

In *Columbia and Richland County: A South Carolina Community 1740-1990*, John Hammond Moore describes the conditions in the city between 1945 and 1954 when only half of the streets within the city limits were paved and about 27 percent of all residential dwellings in the city were considered substandard (one-third lacked running water and half had no inside toilet).

In the circa 1955 painting *Morning on Huger Street* Yaghjian portrays an area that likely represented the physical conditions cited above. The unpaved street defines the foreground for a row of what likely would have been considered substandard housing. The structures are further compromised by the looming "gasometers" of the Columbia Railway Gas & Electric Company, which stood one block south of the homes. Yaghjian's depiction of the site, however, provides a sense of dignity and humanity to the scene. The houses are neatly organized and playfully colorful. Two women wearing aprons and head scarves converse in the foreground adjacent to a vegetable cart. The viewer simply enters into an ordinary day on Huger Street in Columbia.

In this scene, which Yaghjian returned to over and over throughout his career, the artist captures the essence of life in downtown Columbia in the late 19th and early 20th century when a community could be contained within a single frame. All the amenities of daily life are present in one block – residences, a church, a small grocery store and a fresh vegetable cart. Houses are stacked closely together with porches lined up side by side, which later in the day would be populated with neighbors leaning over the rail to talk.

As an artist in Columbia, Yaghjian was particularly interested in African-American neighborhoods, the family-owned corner grocery stores and the individuals who led ordinary lives. The ease and honesty with which he portrayed these subjects reveals a willingness to step across boundaries of race and class that were clearly drawn in Columbia in the 1950s. In doing so, Yaghjian captured elements of the physical and human landscape that

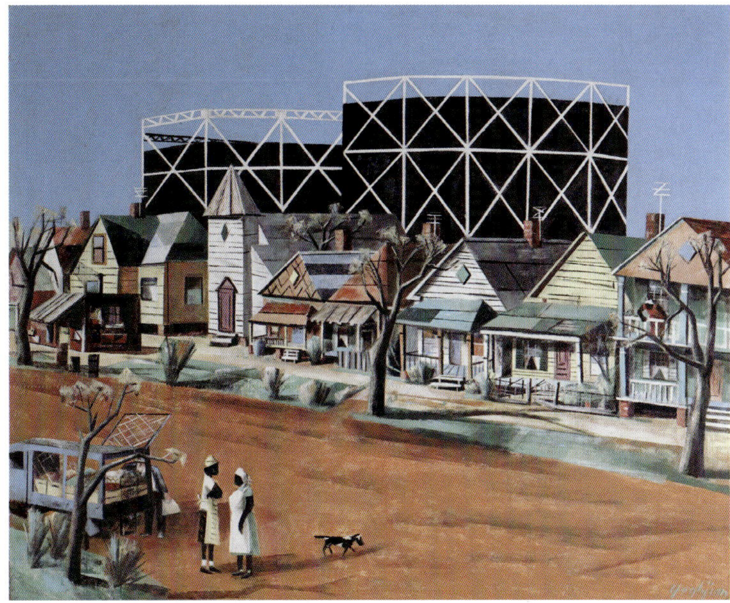

Morning on Huger Street, circa 1955

comprise the fabric of everyday life of often undervalued people and places, that have gone unrecorded.

In the years immediately following Yaghjian's original depictions of Huger Street, the community would change dramatically. In the early 1950s an Urban Rehabilitation Commission convinced the city to enact minimum housing standard and, by 1954 nearly 2,000 substandard units were renovated or demolished. Although the program was city-wide in scope, the campaign concentrated on ten blocks in largely black neighborhoods. "Urban renewal" erased many of the settings from the landscape that Yaghjian depicted. However, for Yaghjian, who was raised in a 19th century clapboard home in an Armenian community, segregated from the larger population of Providence, Rhode Island and whose family was supported by the corner grocery store run by his father and frequented by the immigrants who were just getting by; this scene was familiar, alive and universal.

Robin Waites, Excecutive Director
Historic Columbia Foundation

Edmund Yaghjian

A Selection of Work

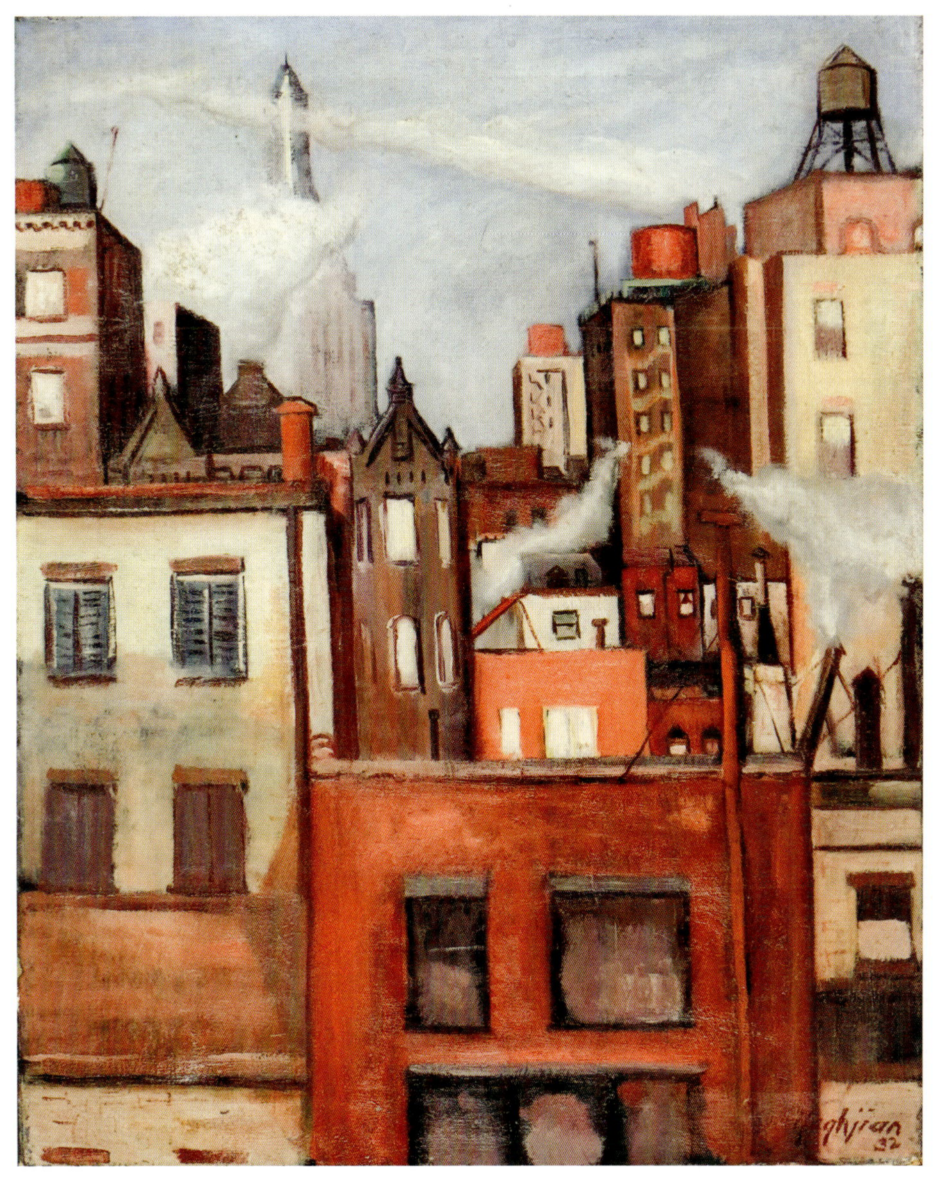

From My Studio on 10th Street, 1932 • Oil on canvas • 25 x 20 • Collection of Candy Yaghjian Waites

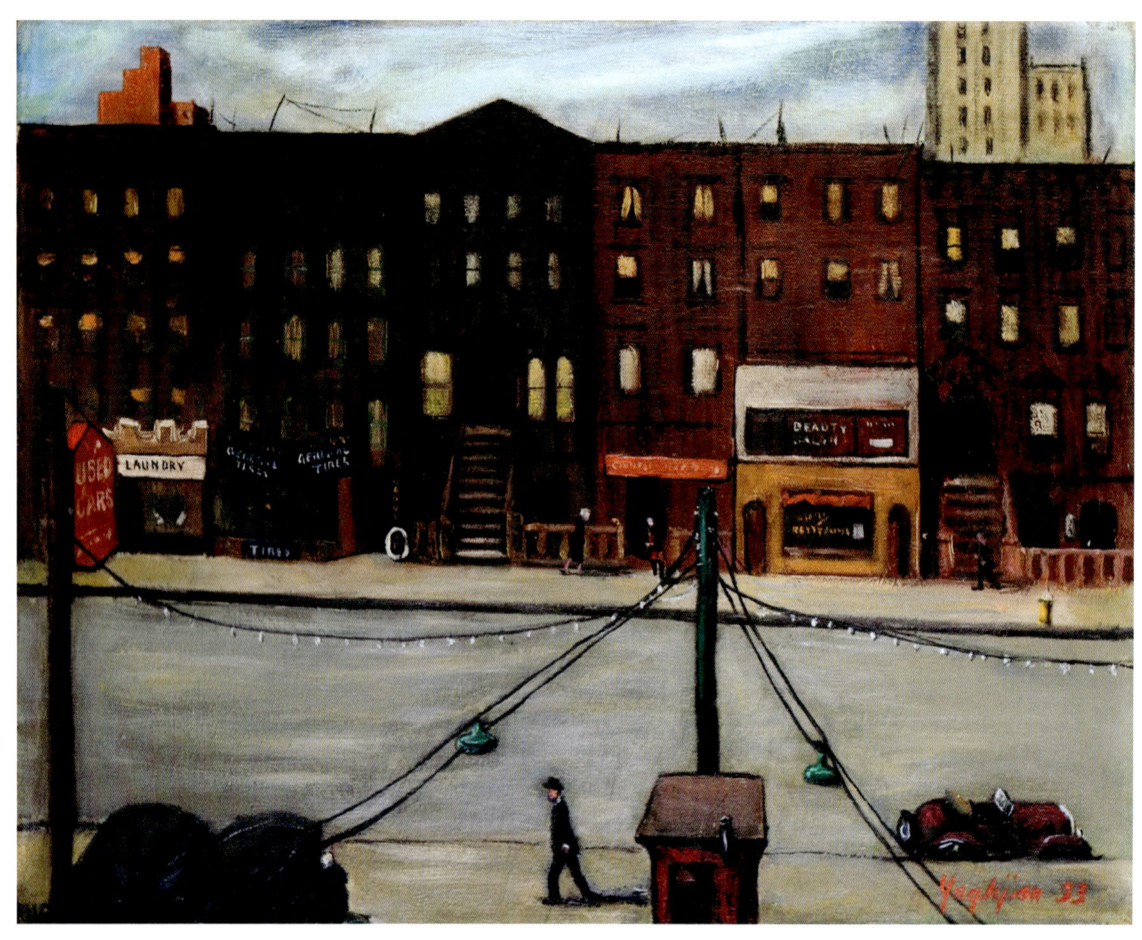

57th Street from My Window, 1933 • Oil on canvas • 16 x 20 • Collection of David H. Yaghjian

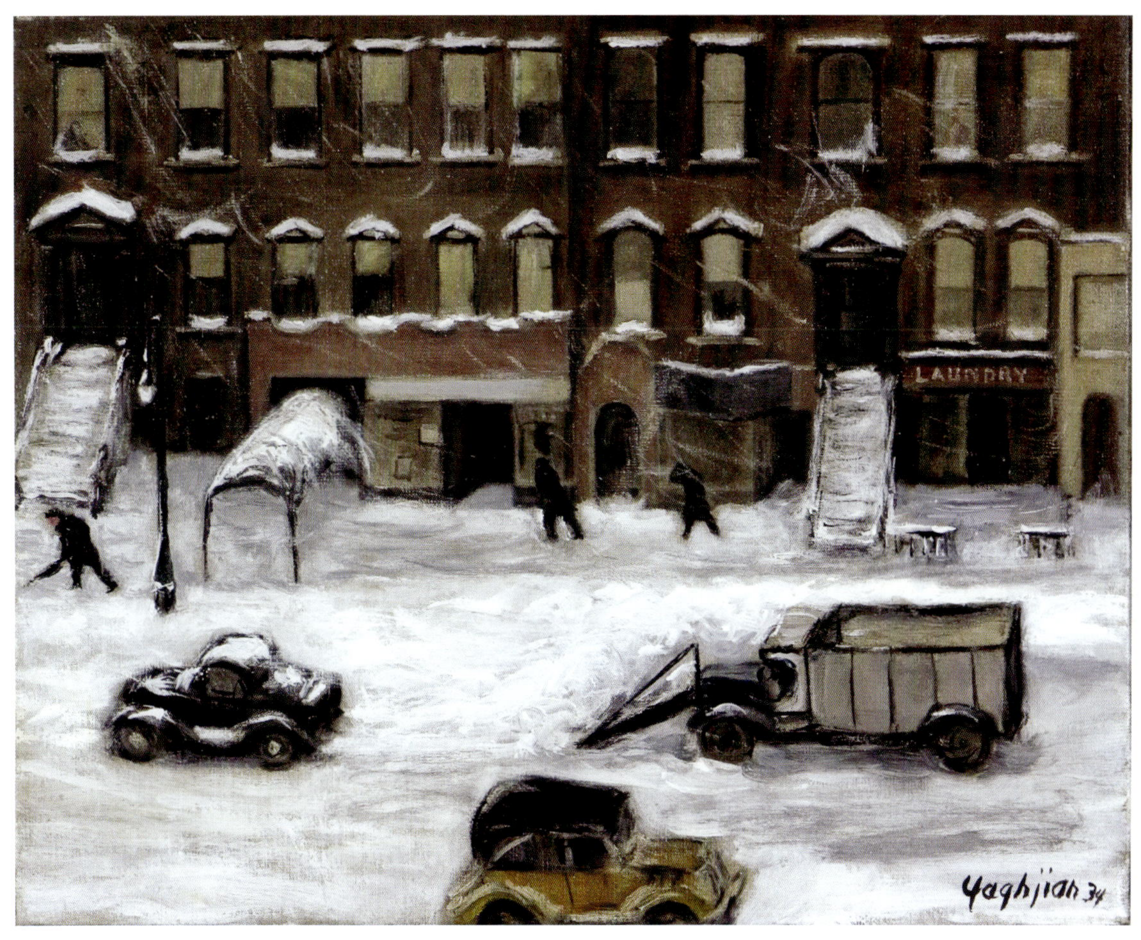

Snow on 56th Street, 1934 • Oil on canvas • 16 x 20 • Collection of David H. Yaghjian

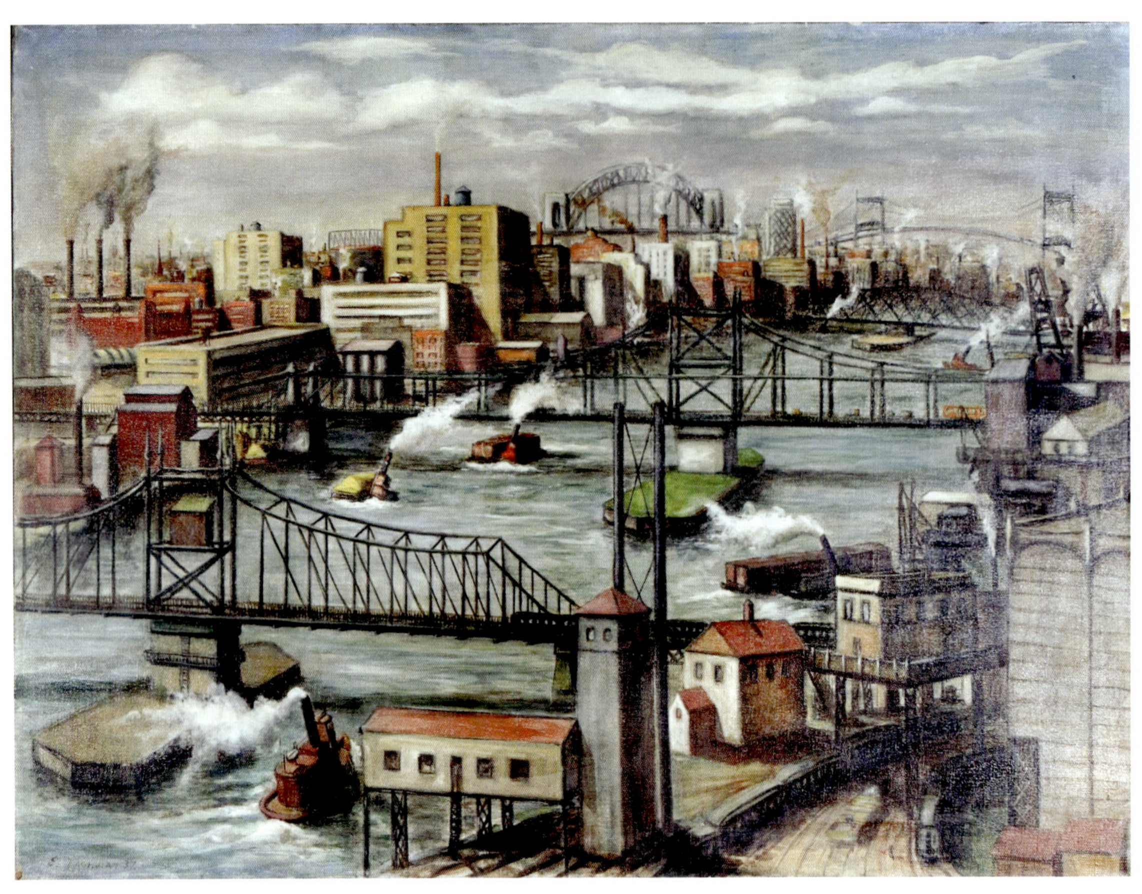

Tugboats on the East River, 1937 • Oil on canvas • 24 x 36 • Collection of Candy Yaghjian Waites

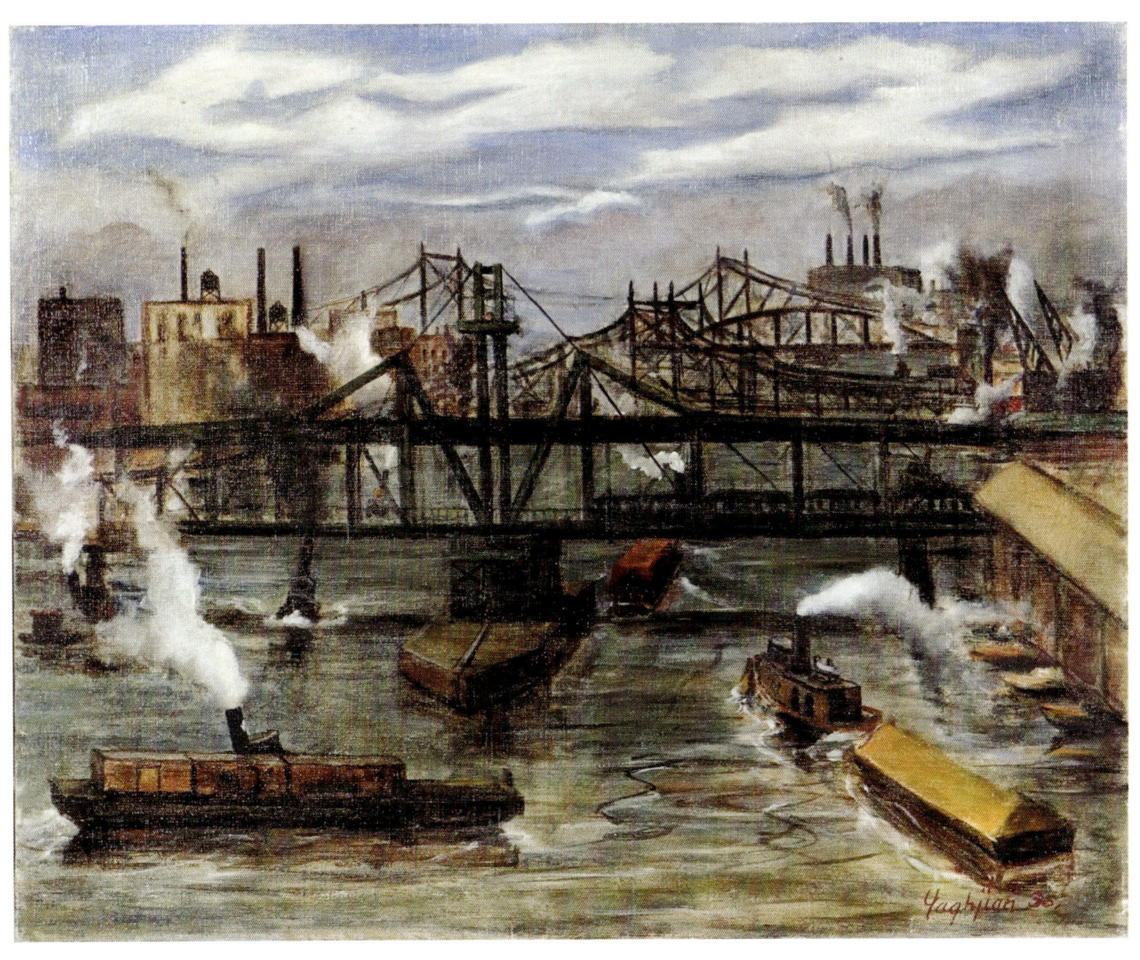

Bridges on the East River, 1936 • Oil on canvas • 20 x 25 • Collection of David H. Yaghjian

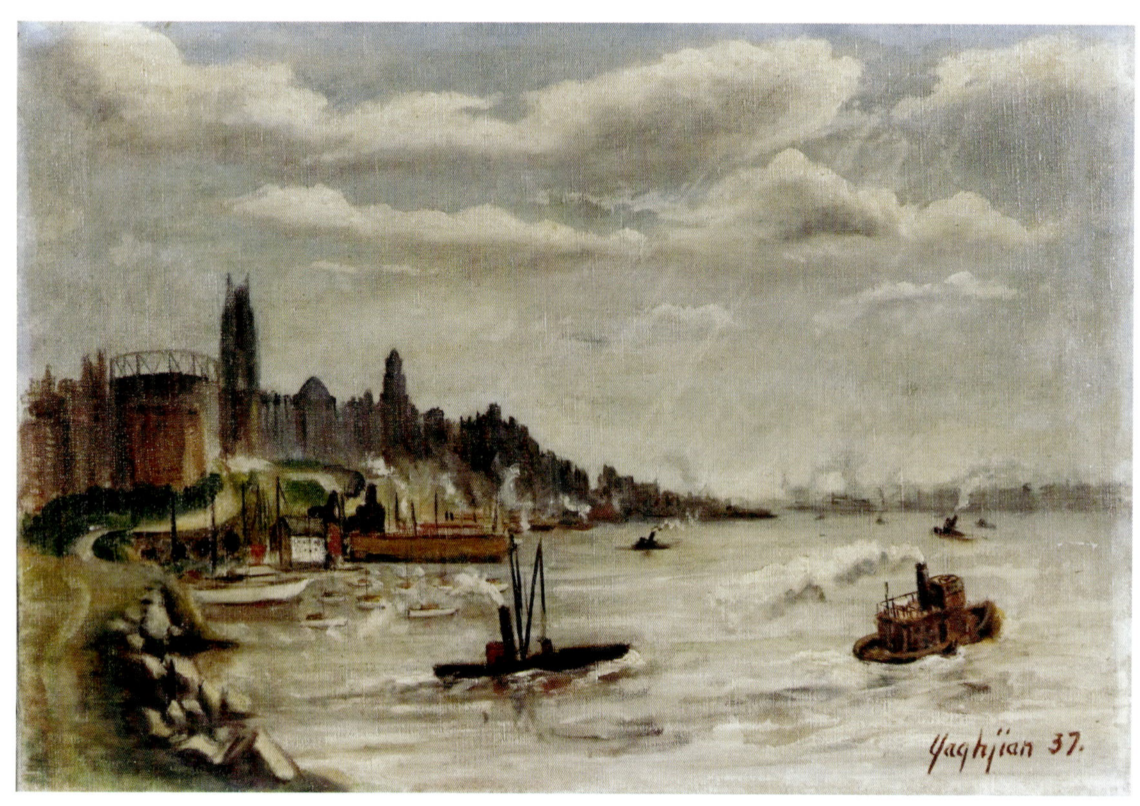

Looking Down the Hudson, 1937 • Oil on canvas • 16 x 24 • Collection of Susan A Yaghjian

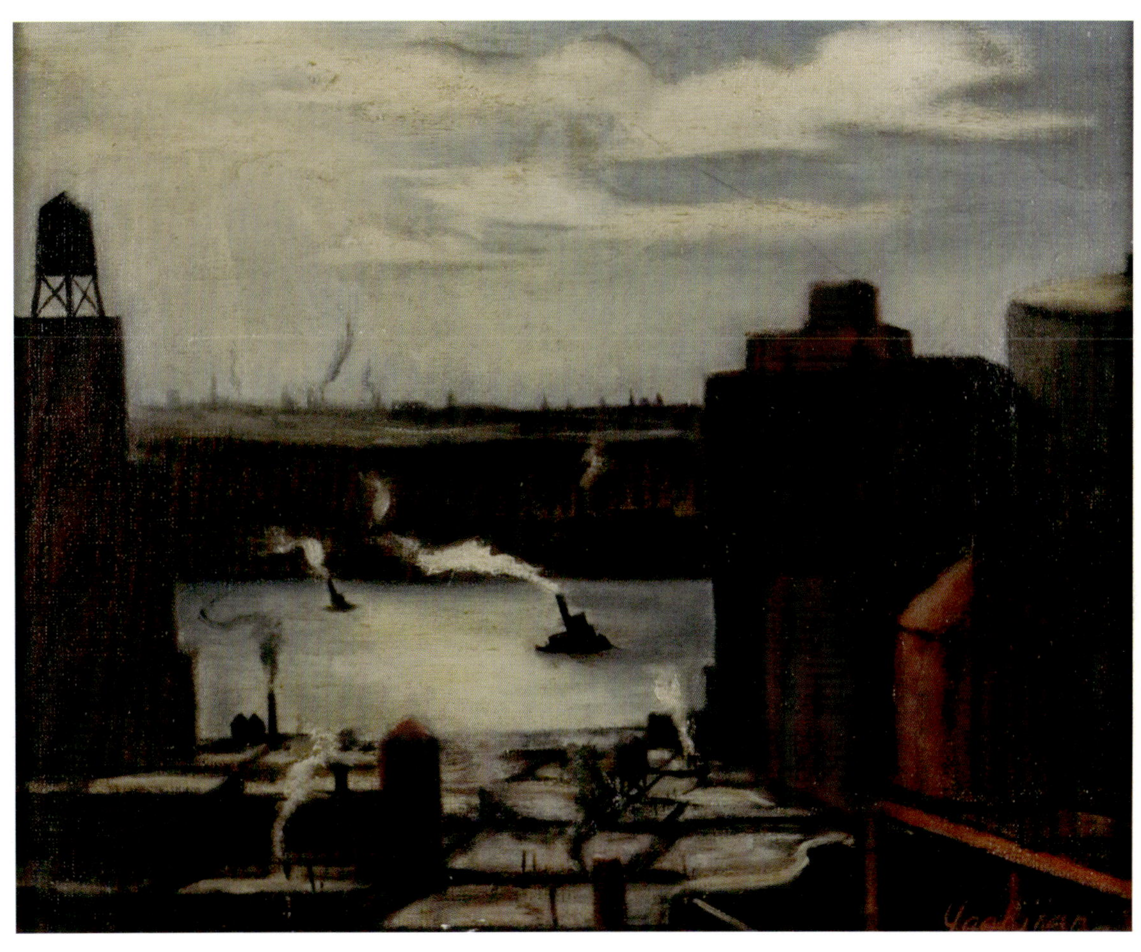

Across to Jersey, 1935 • Oil on board • 14 x 17 • Collection of Candy Yaghjian Waites

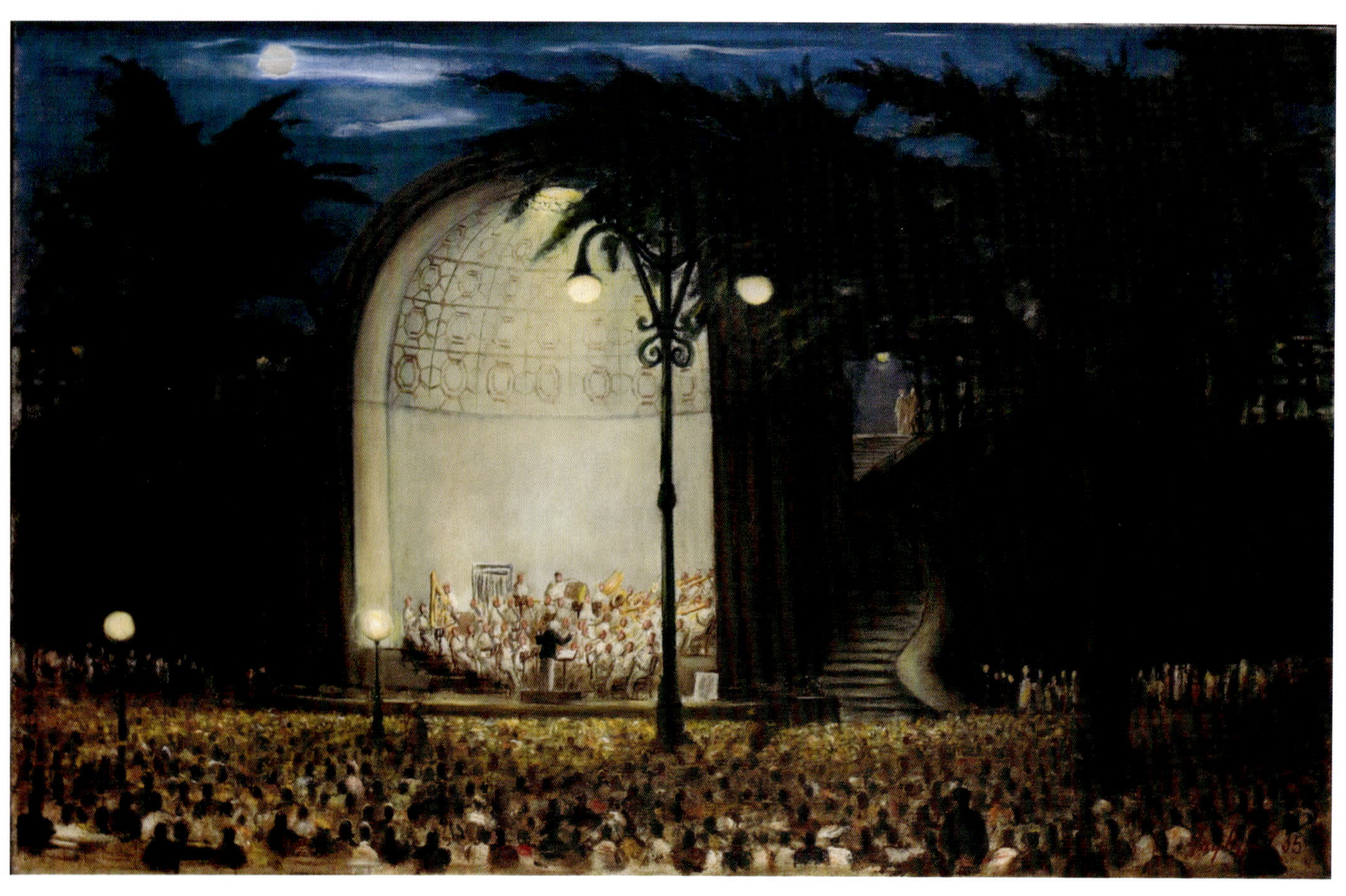

Goldman's Band in Central Park, 1935 • Oil on canvas • 24 x 38 • Collection of David H. Yaghjian

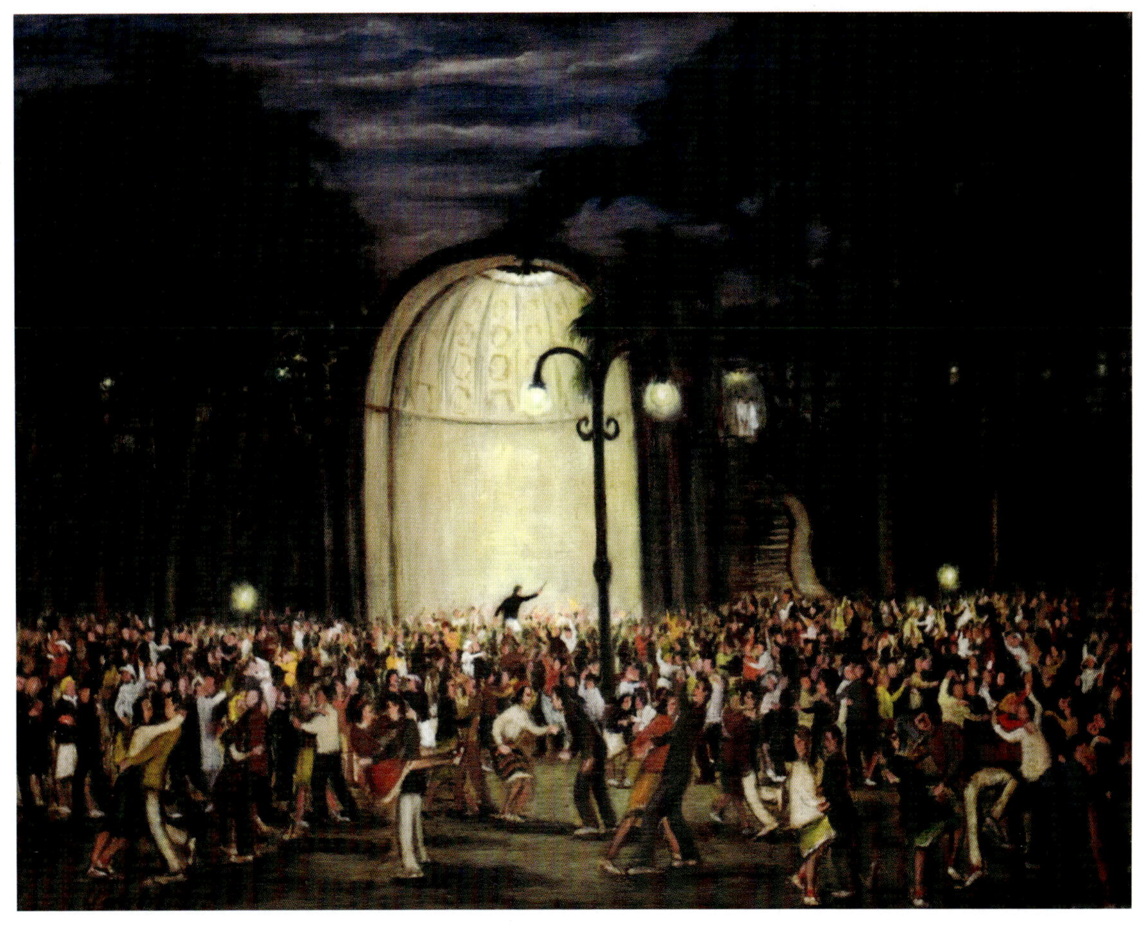

Jitterbugging on the Mall, 1938 • Oil on canvas • 22 x 28 • Private collection

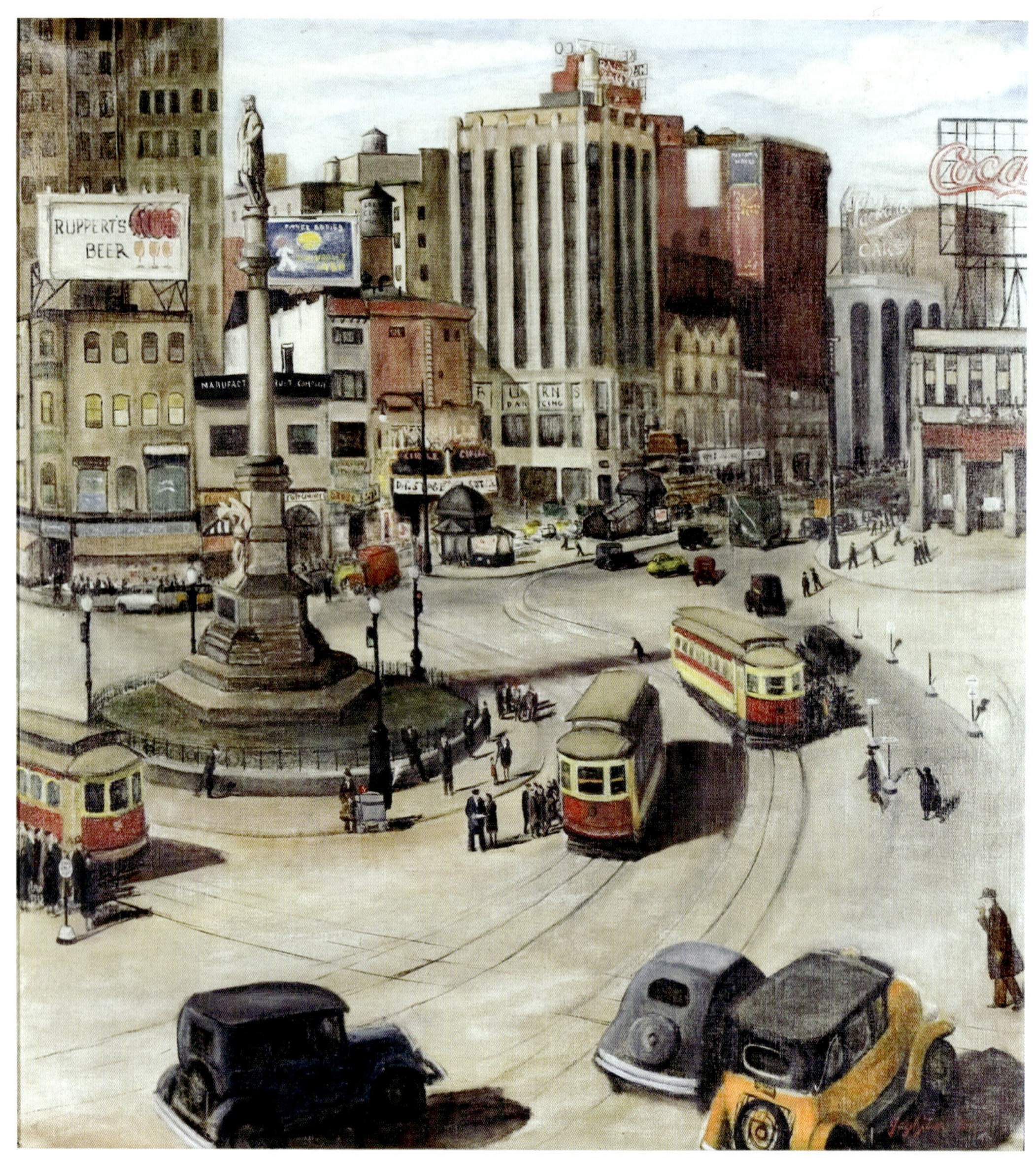

Columbus Circle, 1934 • Oil on board • 36 x 33 • Collection of Candy Yaghjian Waites

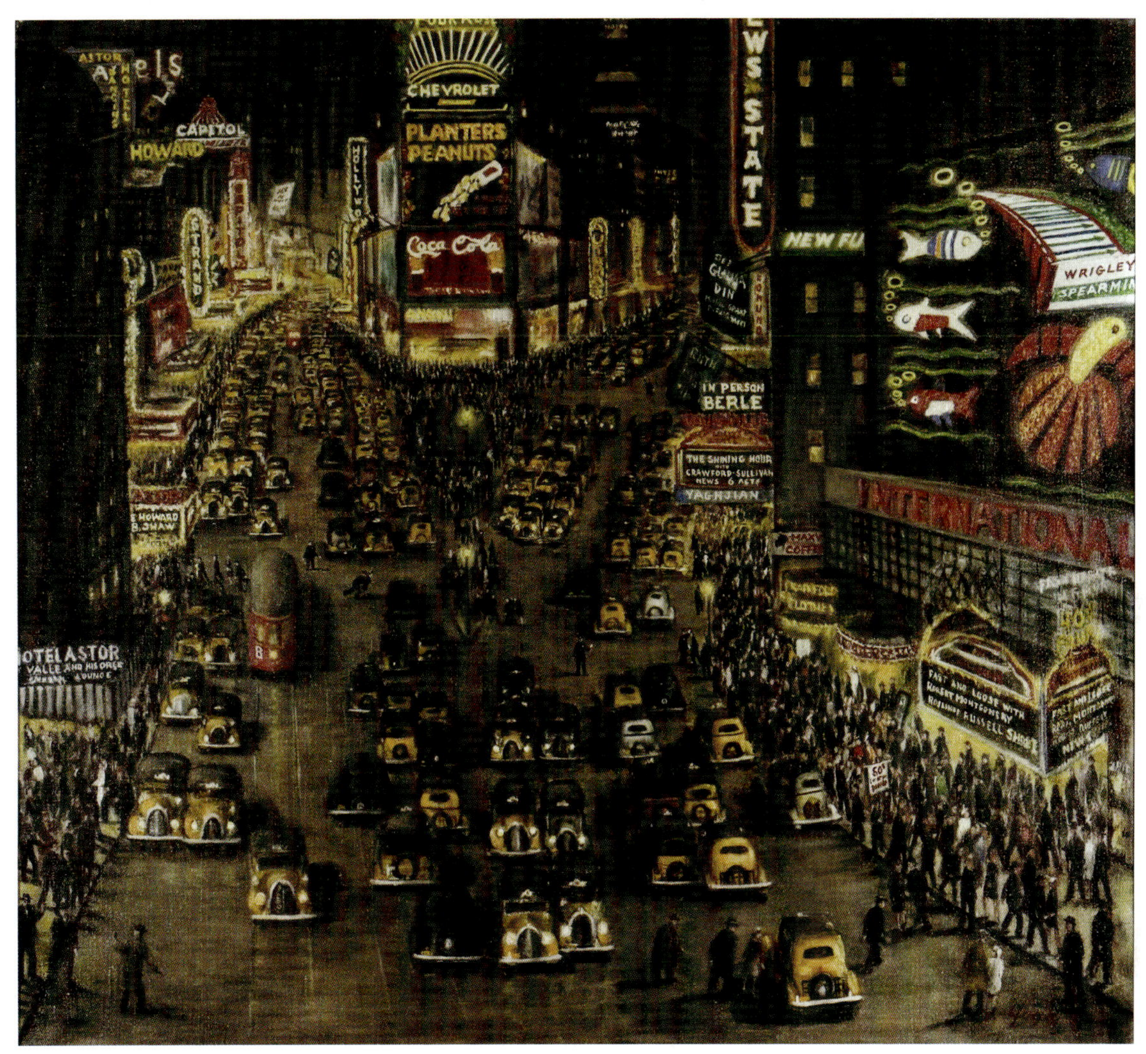

Times Square, circa 1935 • Oil on canvas • 36 x 40 • On loan from the Estate of Dorothy Candy Yaghjian

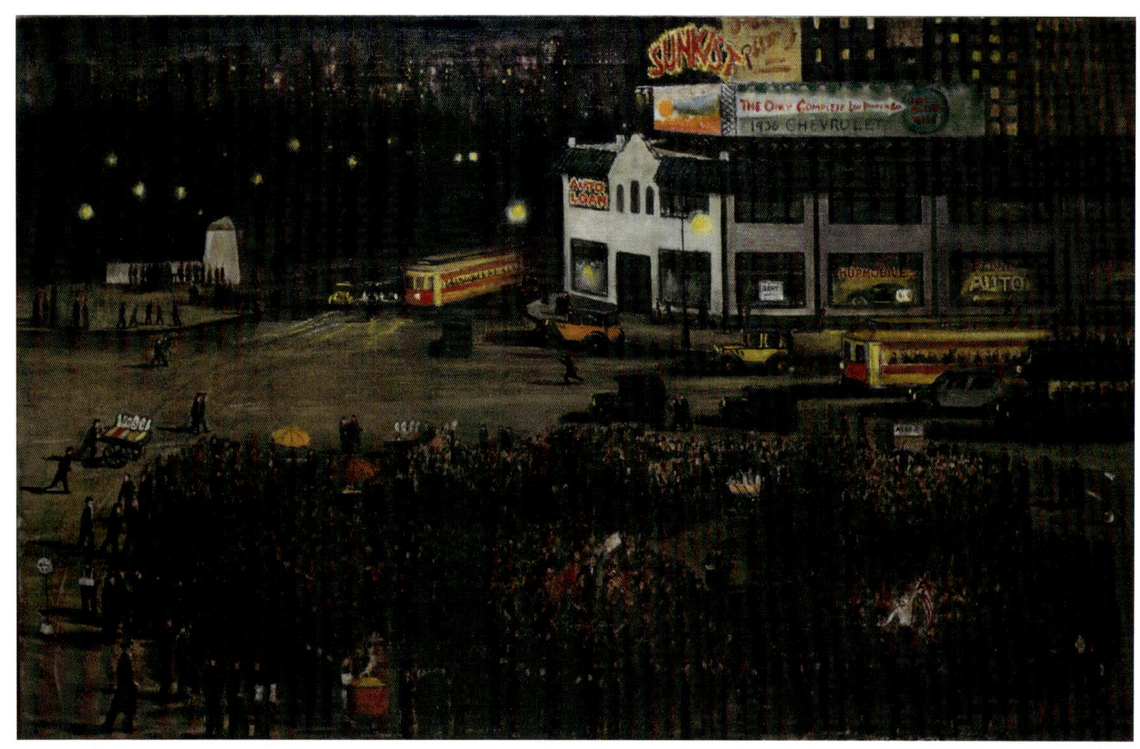

Most Any Night on Columbus Circle, 1935 • Oil on canvas • 24 x 38 • On loan from the Estate of Dorothy Candy Yaghjian

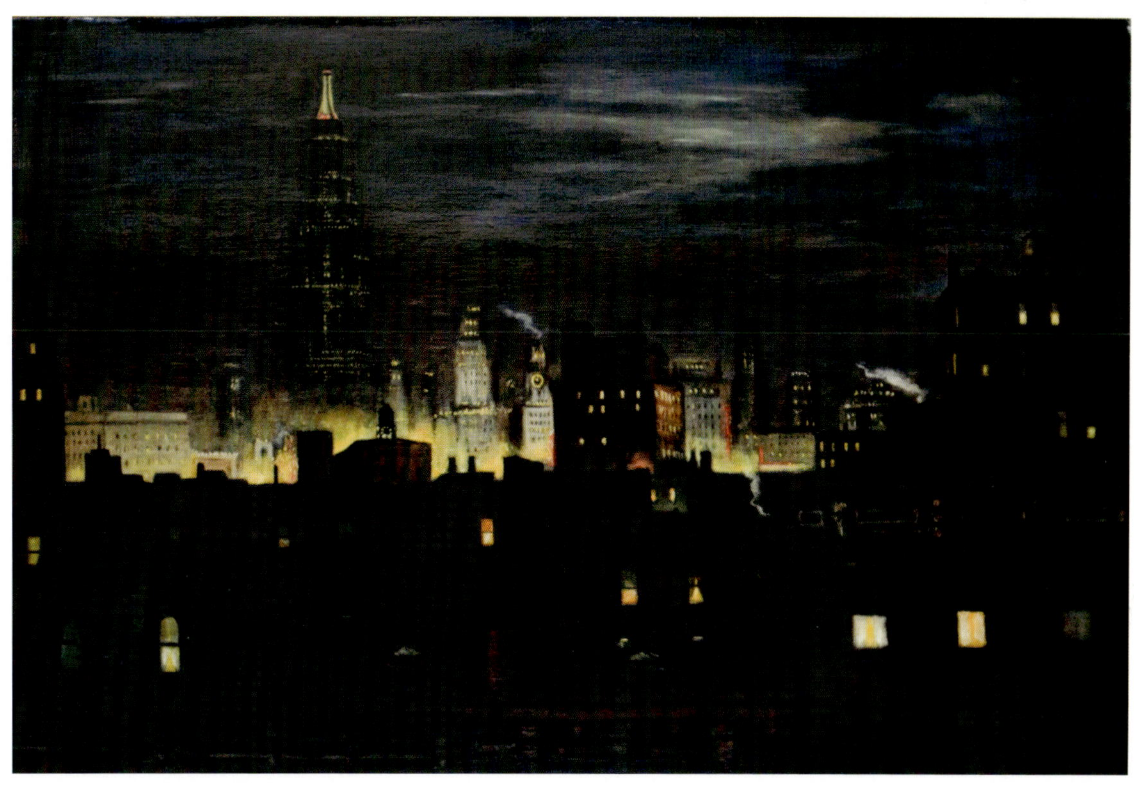

Night in Manhattan, 1936 • Oil on board • 24 x 36 • On loan from the Estate of Dorothy Candy Yaghjian

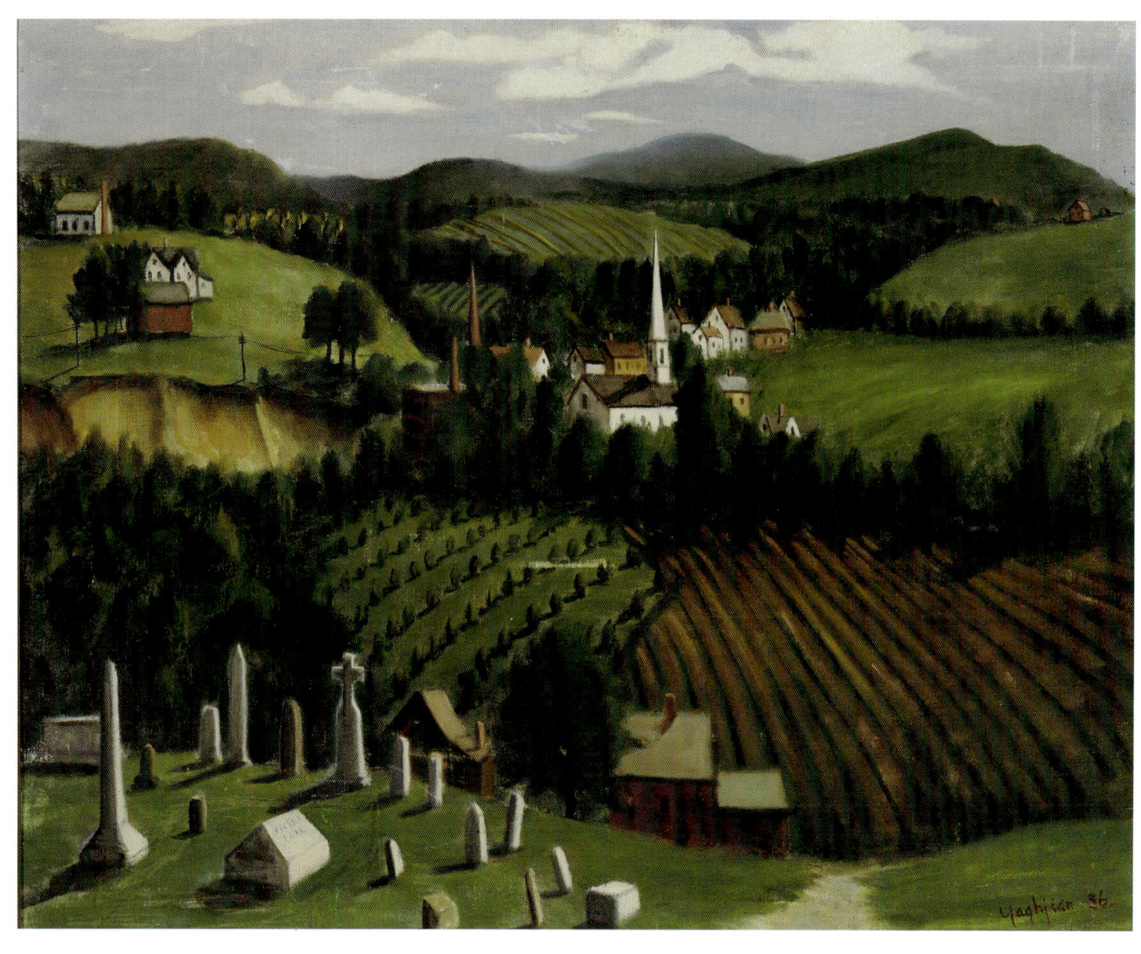

The White Church, 1936 • Oil on canvas • 23 7/8 x 30 • Smithsonian American Art Museum

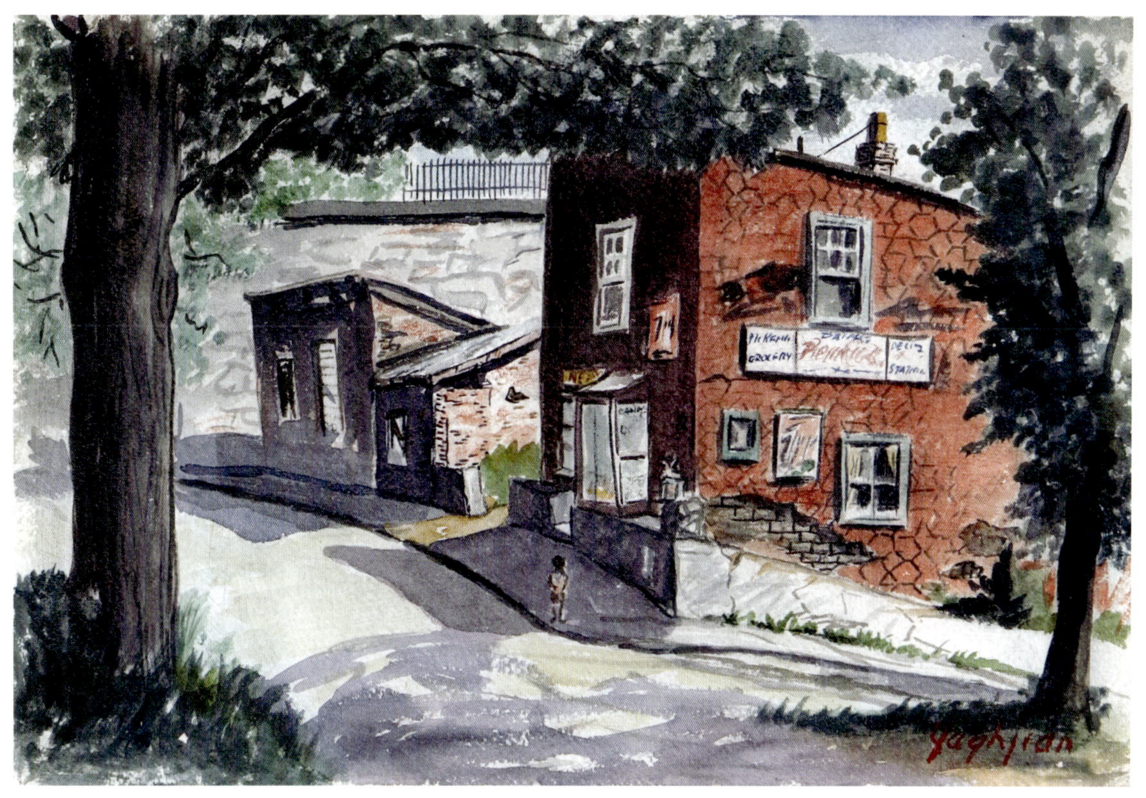

Red Store in Ossining, New York, 1943 • Watercolor on paper • 11 ½ x 16 ¼ • Private collection

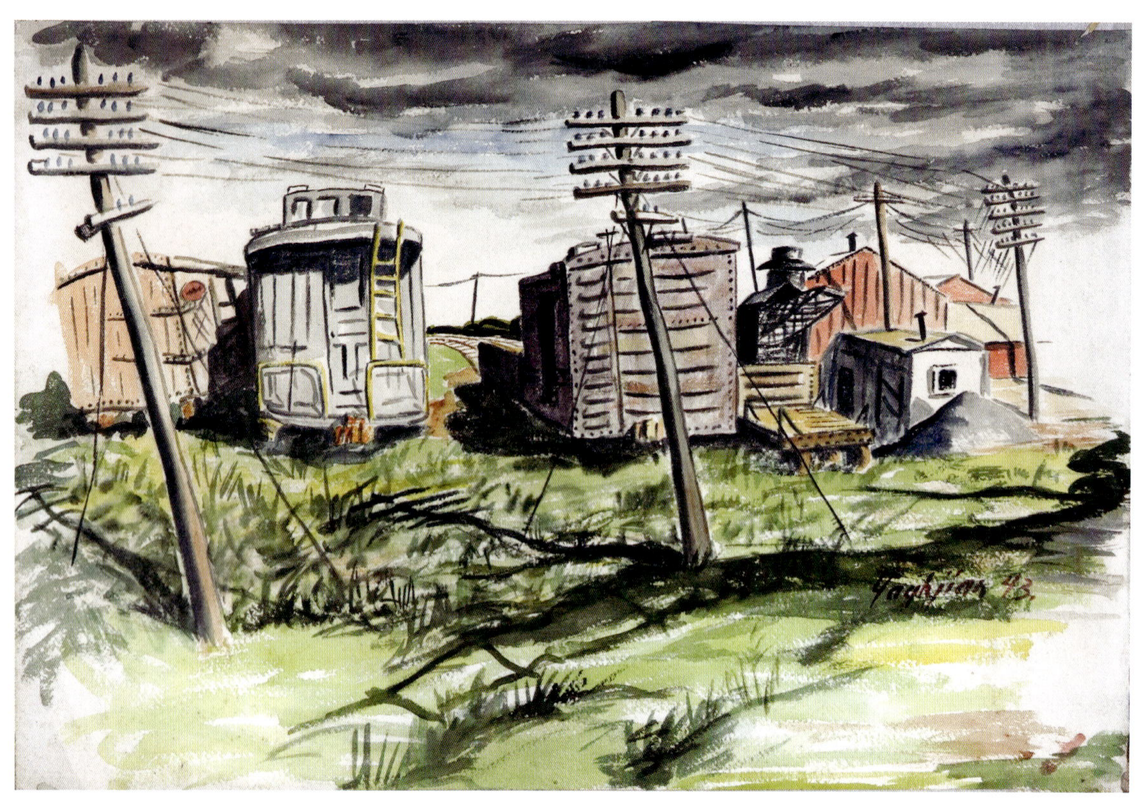

Untitled (Ossining, New York), 1943 • Watercolor on paper • 16 ½ x 21 ¾ • Private collection

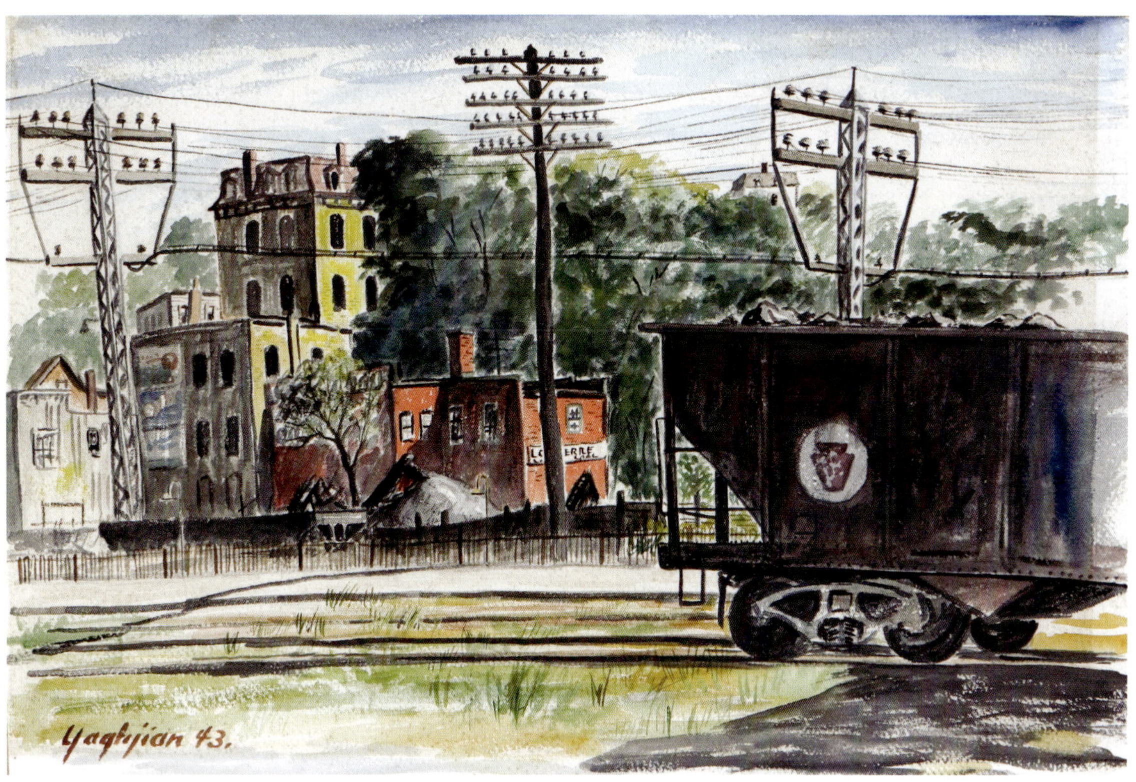

Coal Cars in Ossining, New York, 1943 • Watercolor on paper • 15 ½ x 22 ¾ • Private collection

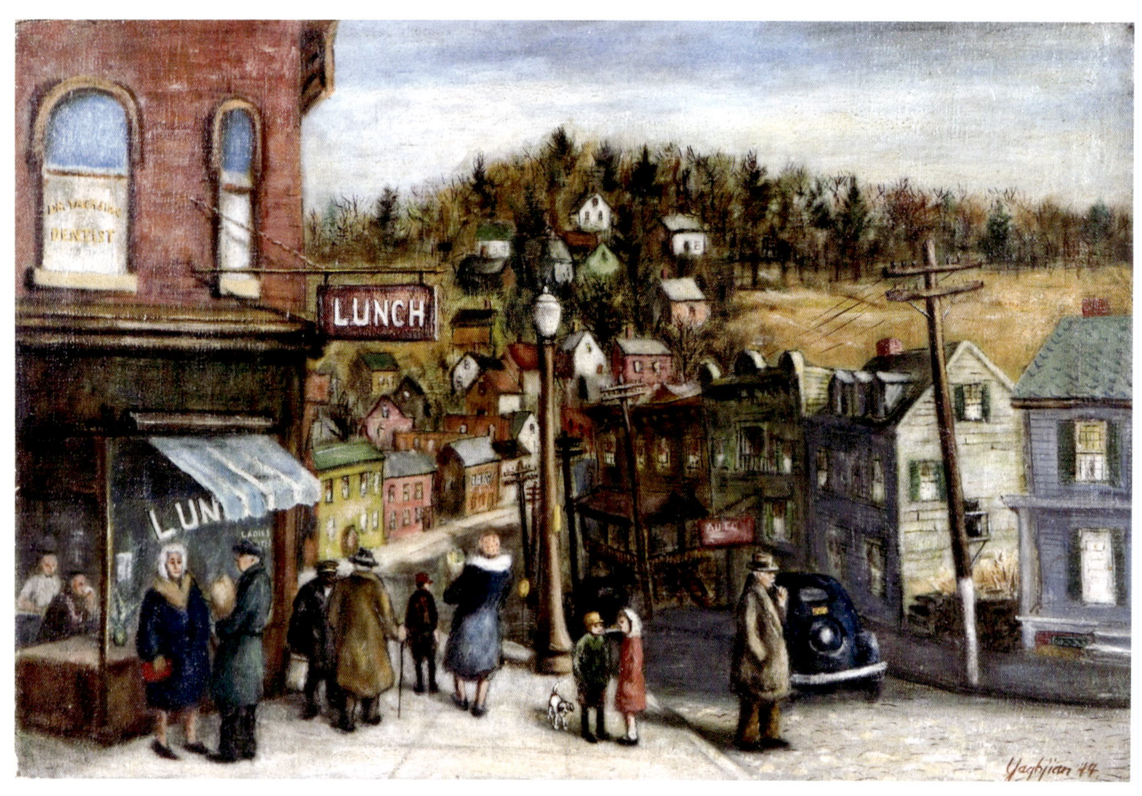

Ossining, 1944 • Oil on canvas • 20 x 30 • Collection of Susan A. Yaghjian

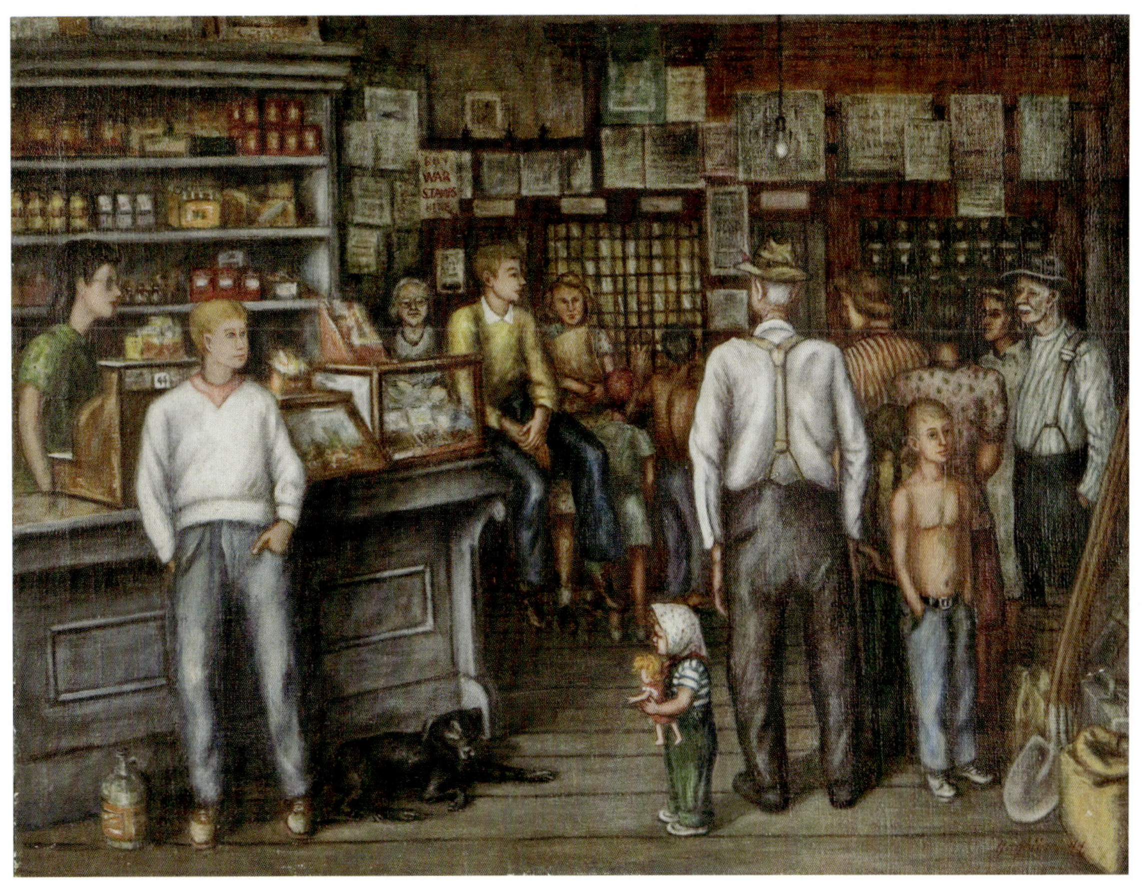

Candy and Mother Waiting for the Mail, 1944 • Oil on canvas • 25 x 33 • Collection of Candy Yaghjian Waites

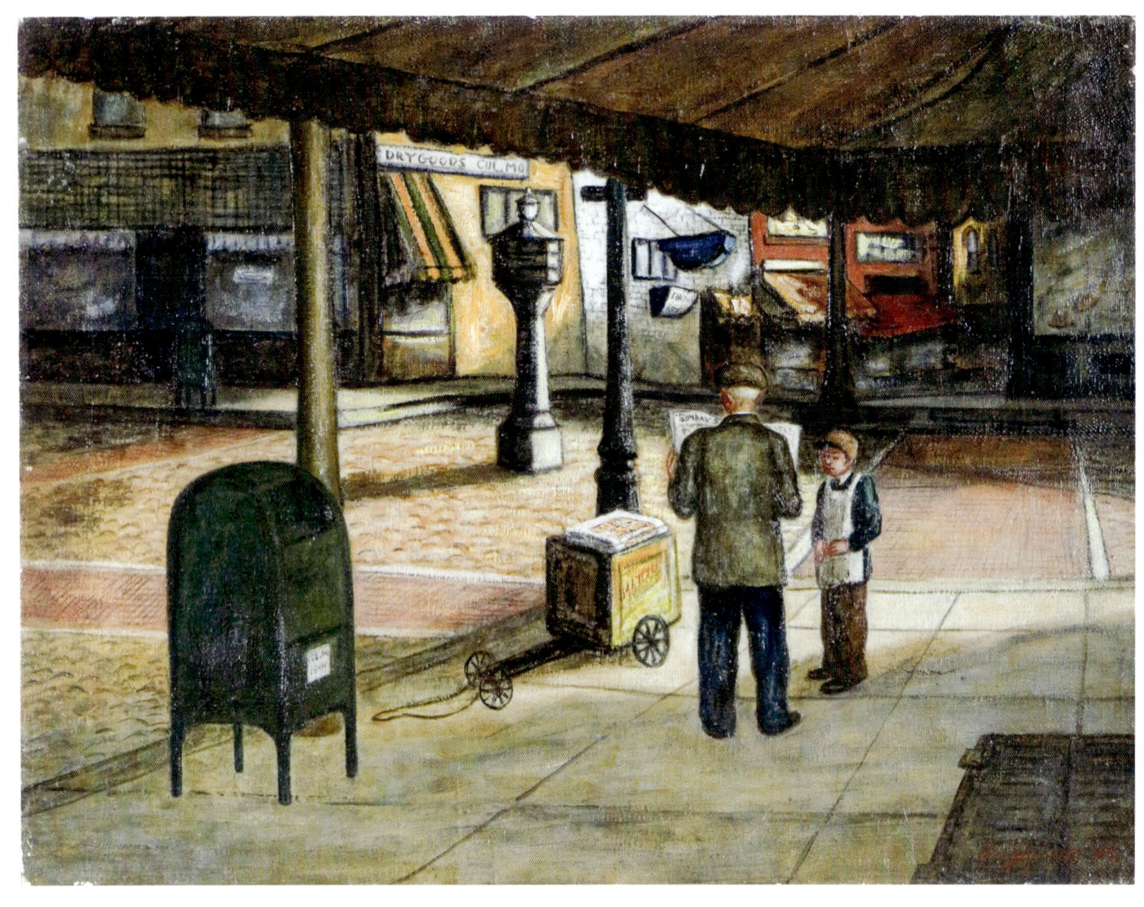

Sunday Papers, 1944 • Oil on canvas •18 x 24 • Collection of David H. Yaghjian

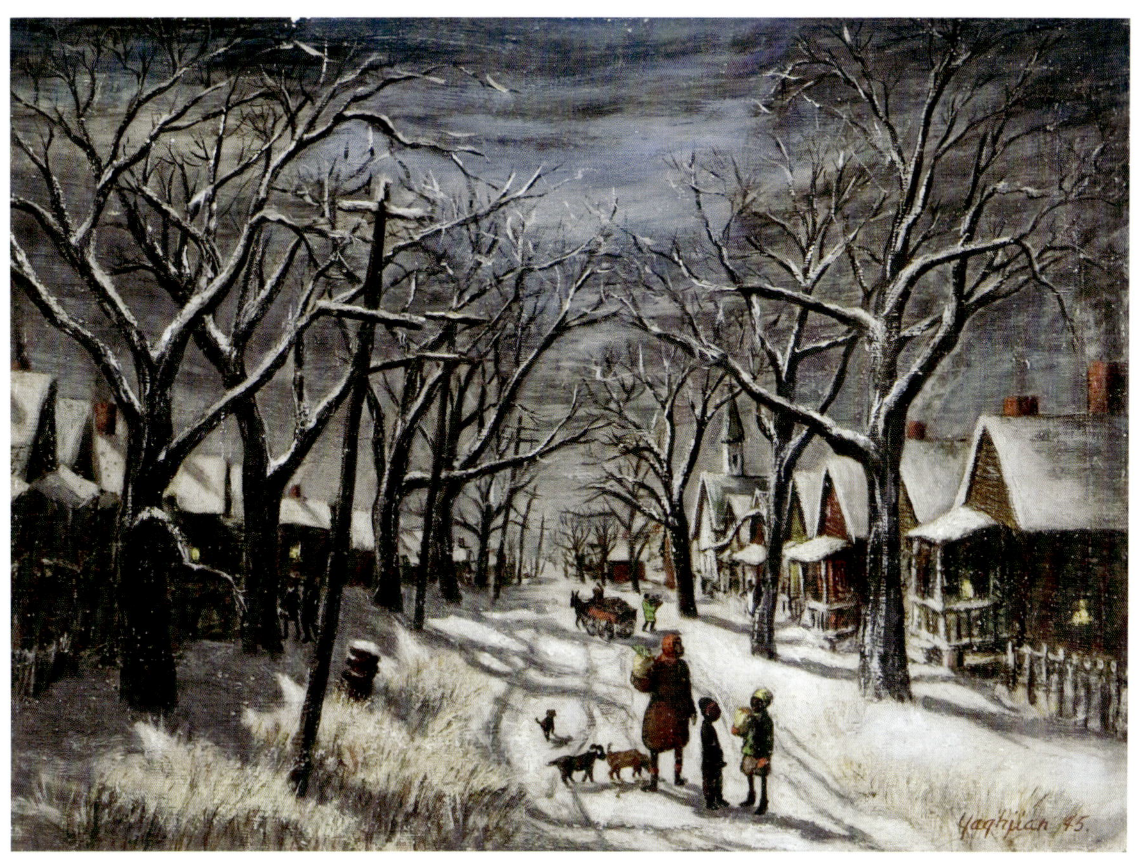

Returning Home from the Groceries, 1945 • Oil on board • Size 15 x 21 • Collection of Susan A. Yaghjian

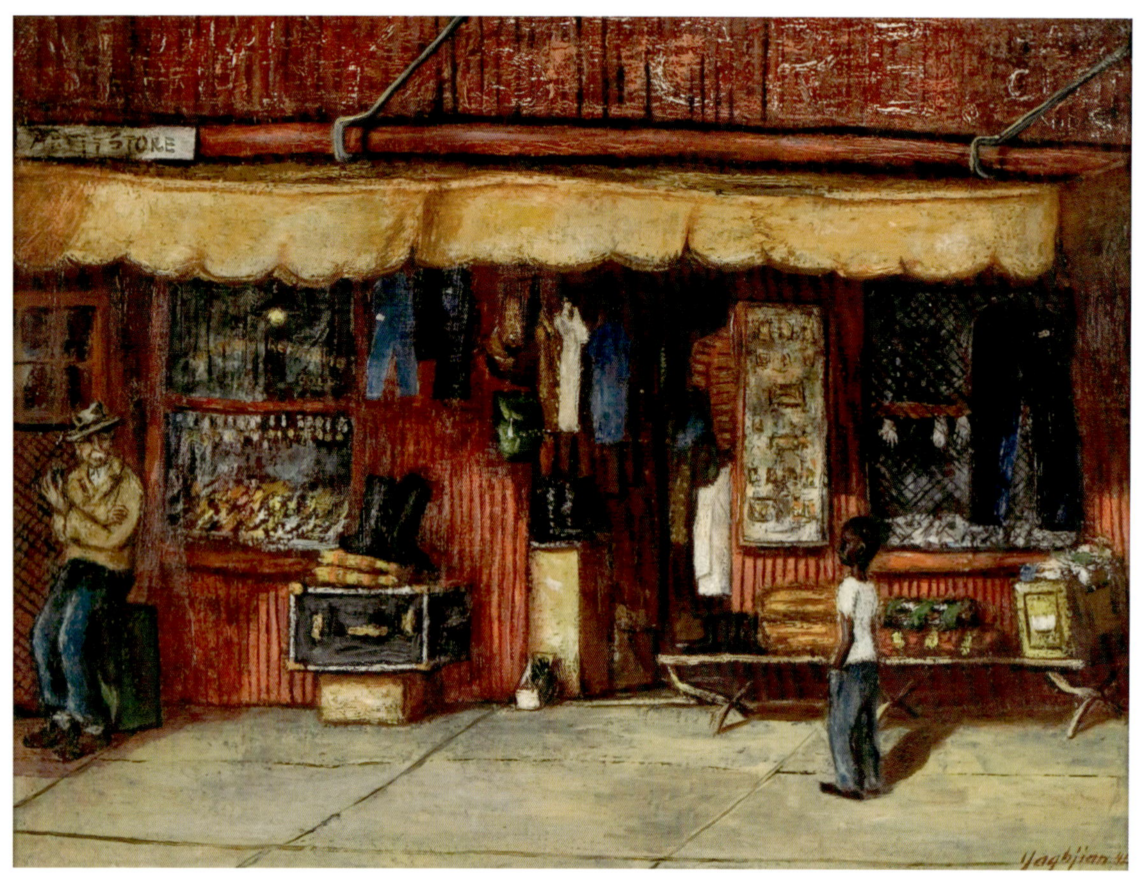

Army Store, 1946 • Oil on canvas • 18 x 24 • Collection of David Hodges

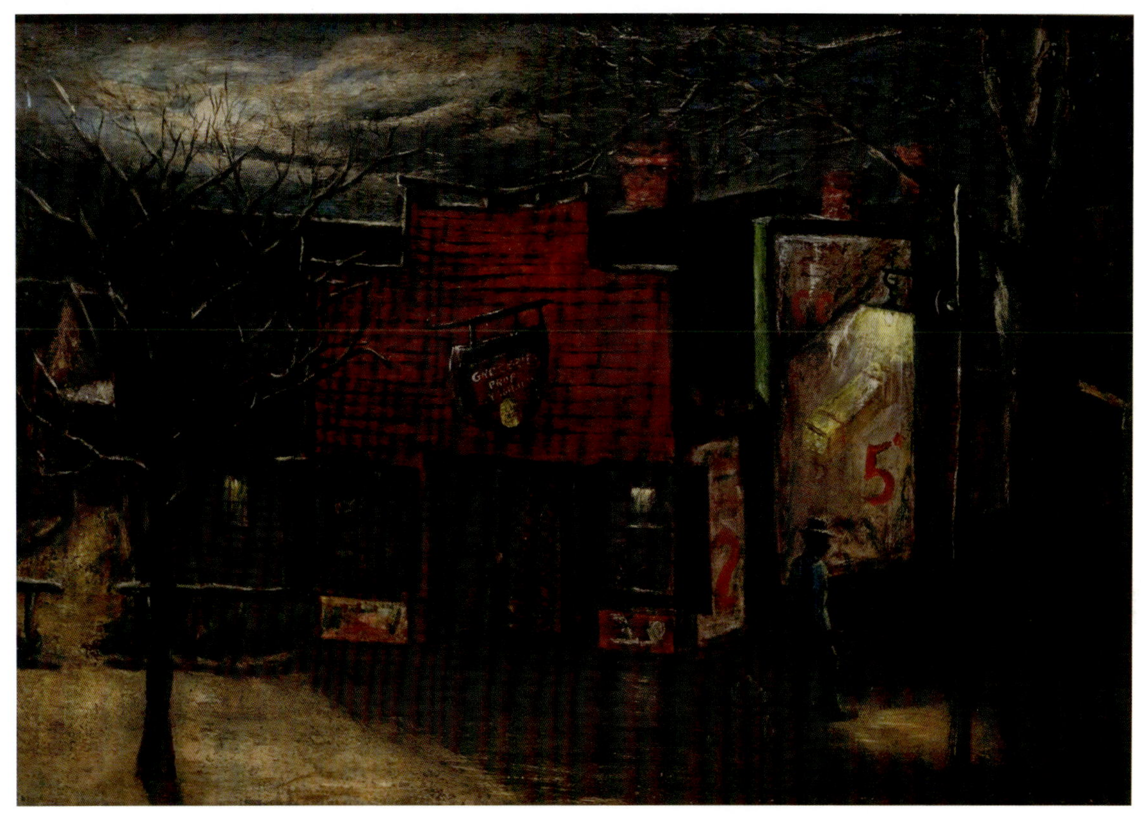

Night on Assembly Street, circa 1946 • Oil on board • 17 ¾ x 26 • Collection of Candy Yaghjian Waites

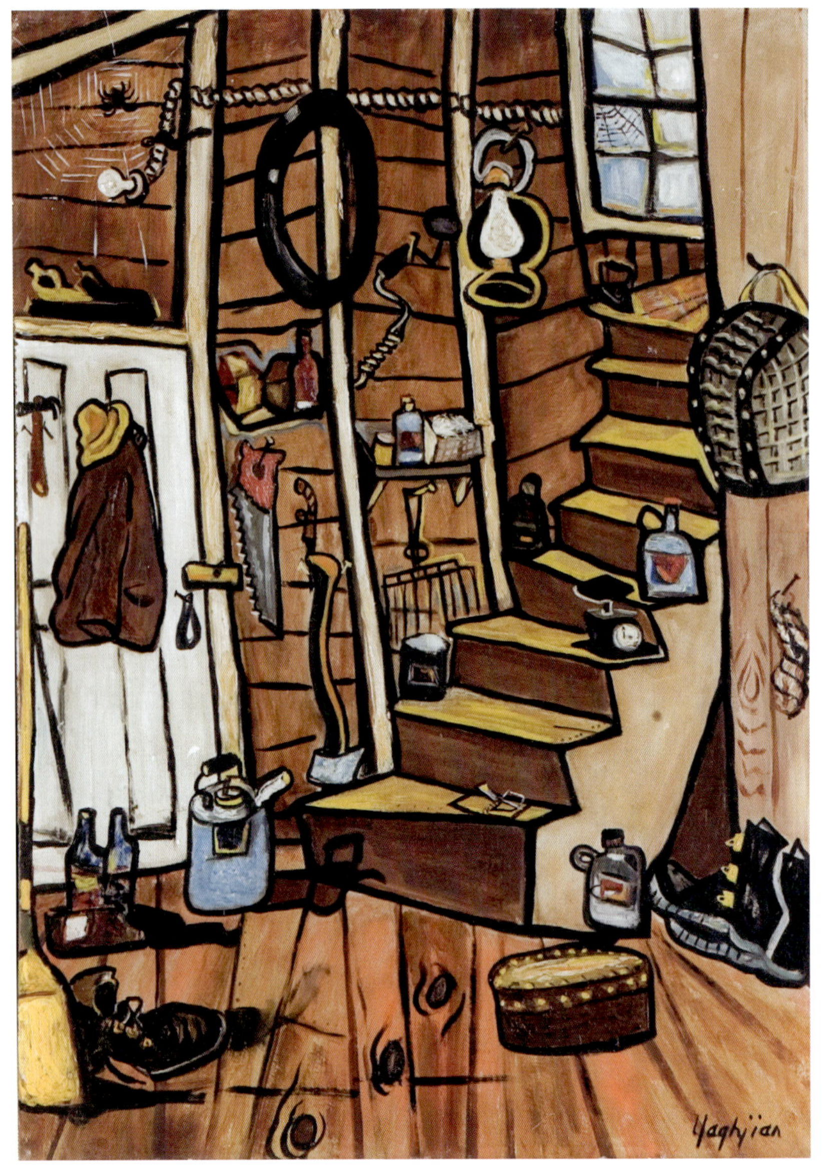

Back Stairs in Vermont, 1949 • Oil on board • 24 x 17 • Collection of Candy Yaghjian Waites

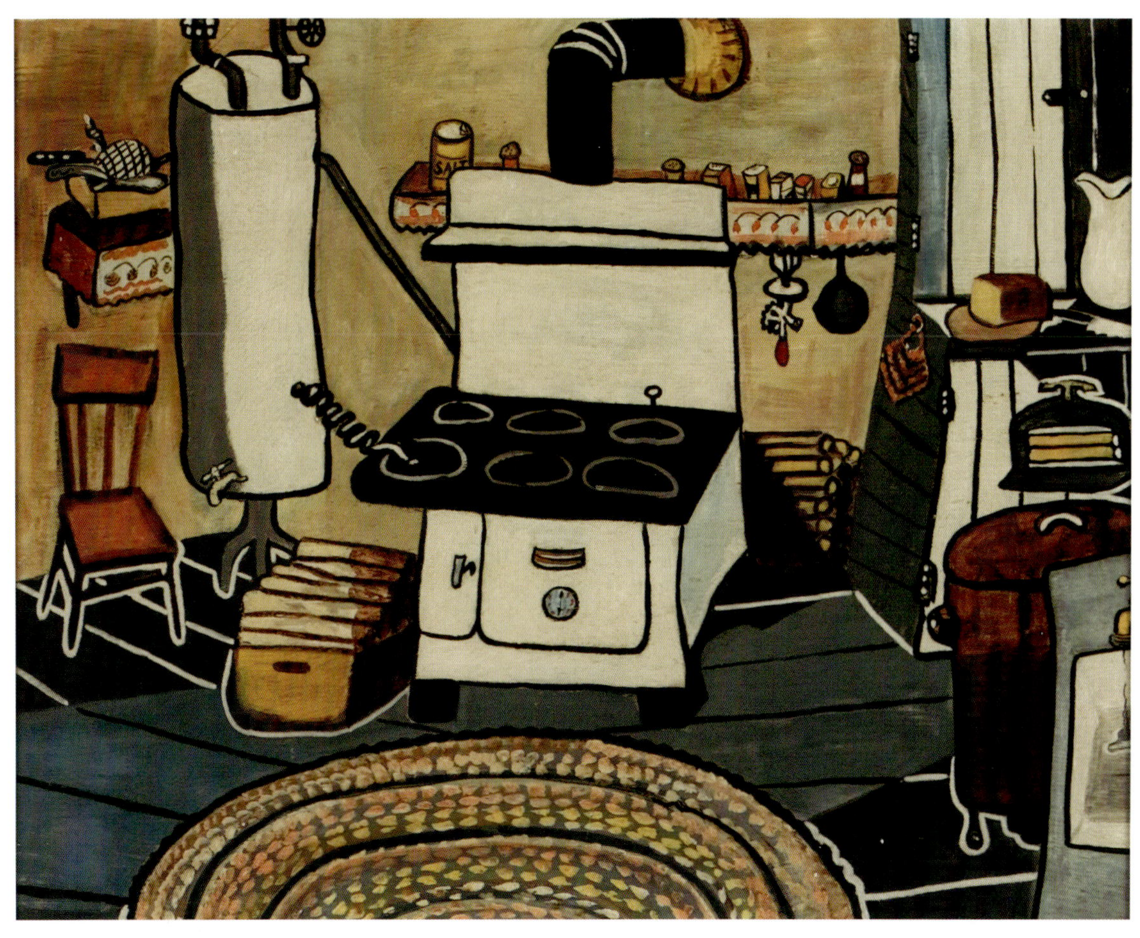

Kitchen in Wallingford, 1949 • Oil on canvas • 16 x 20 • Collection of David H. Yaghjian

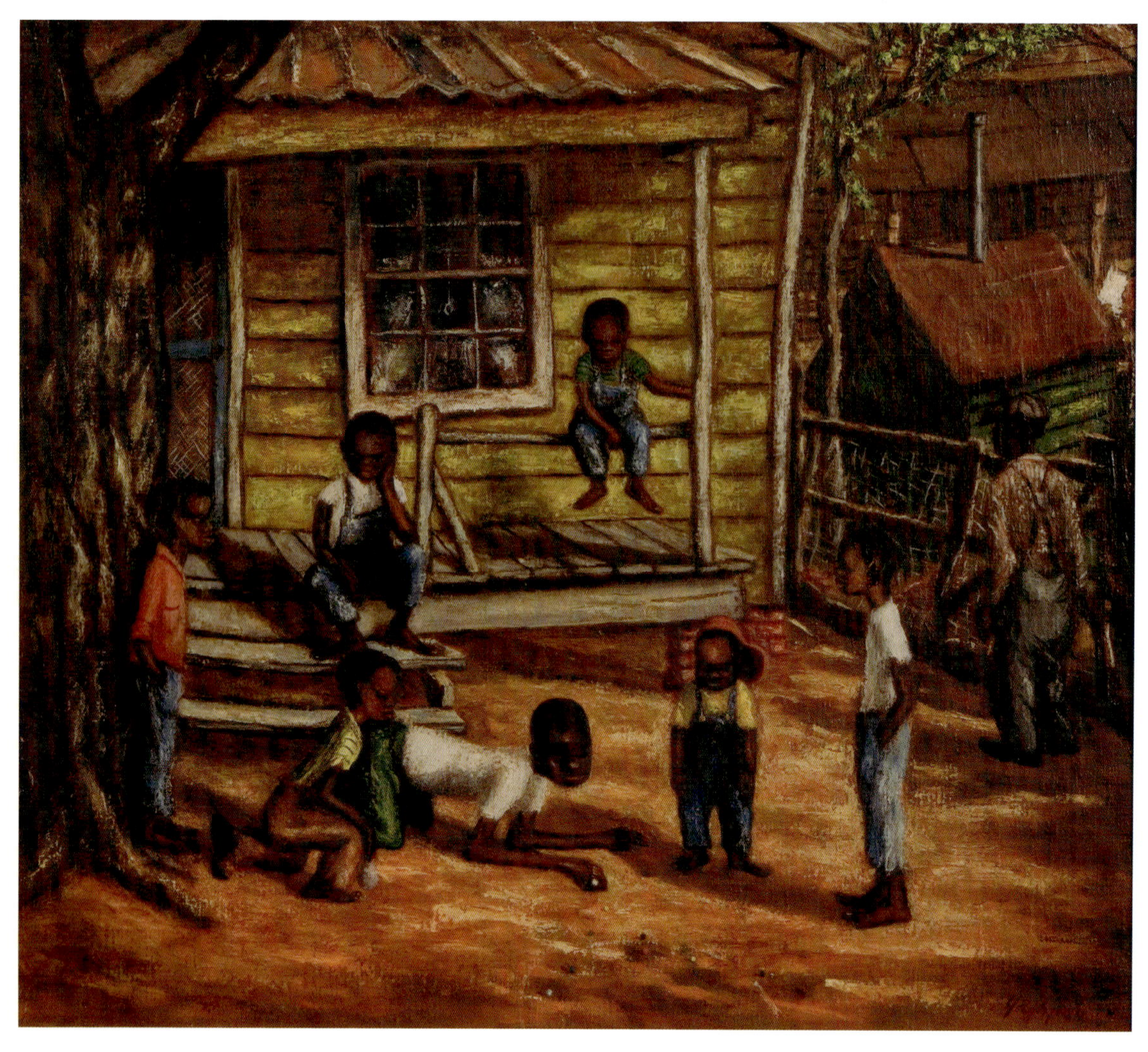

The Champ, 1949 • Oil on canvas • 27 ¼ x 31• Collection of Donald Kurtz

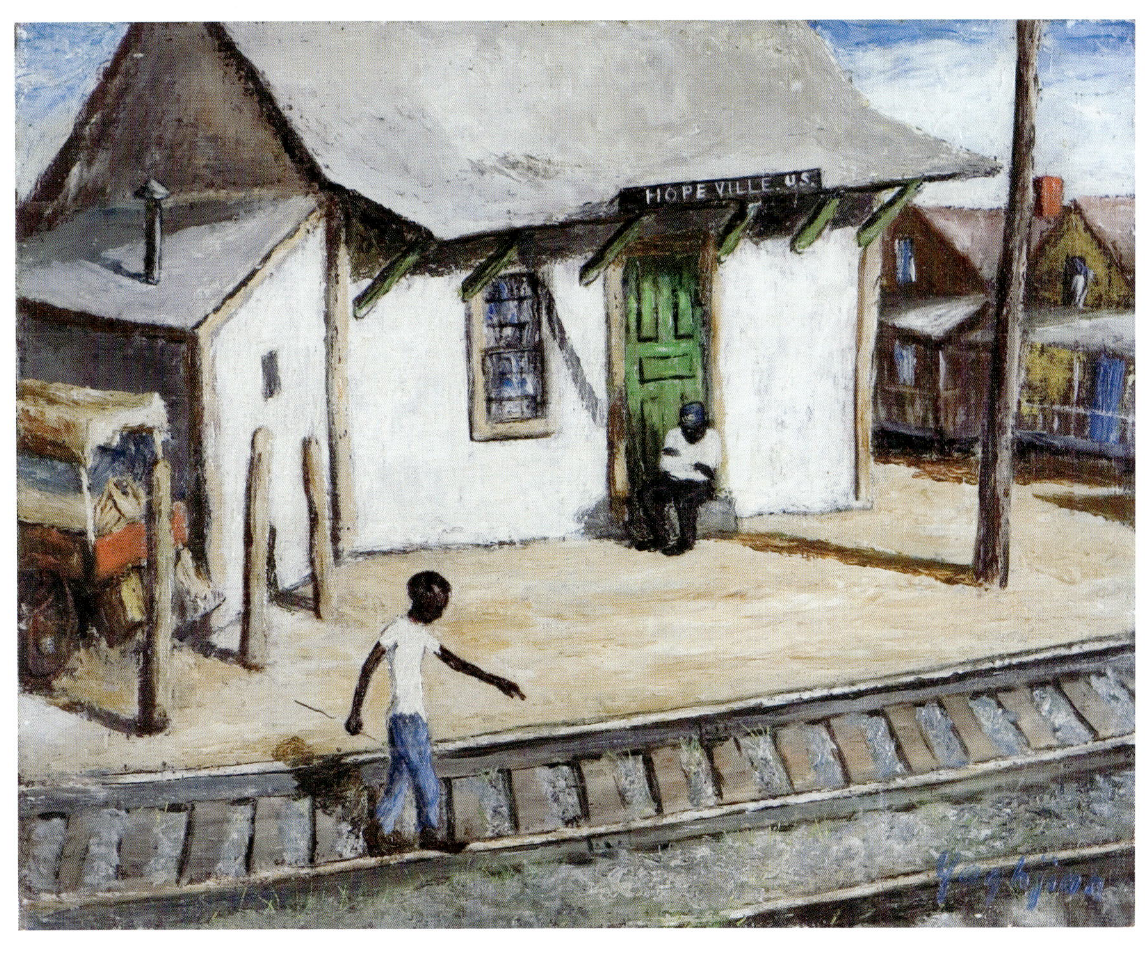

Hopeville, circa 1948 • Oil on canvas on board • 16 x 20 • Private Collection

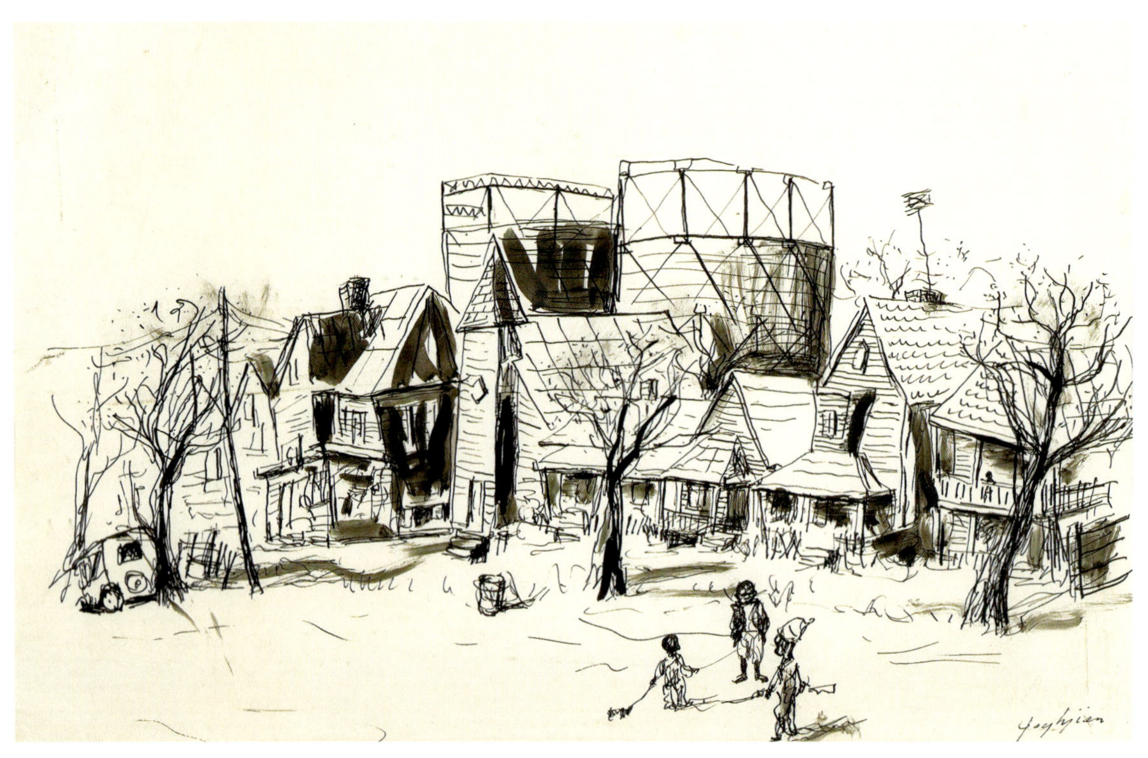

Water Tower #1, circa 1950 • Ink on paper • 13 ½ x 21 ½ • Columbia Museum of Art

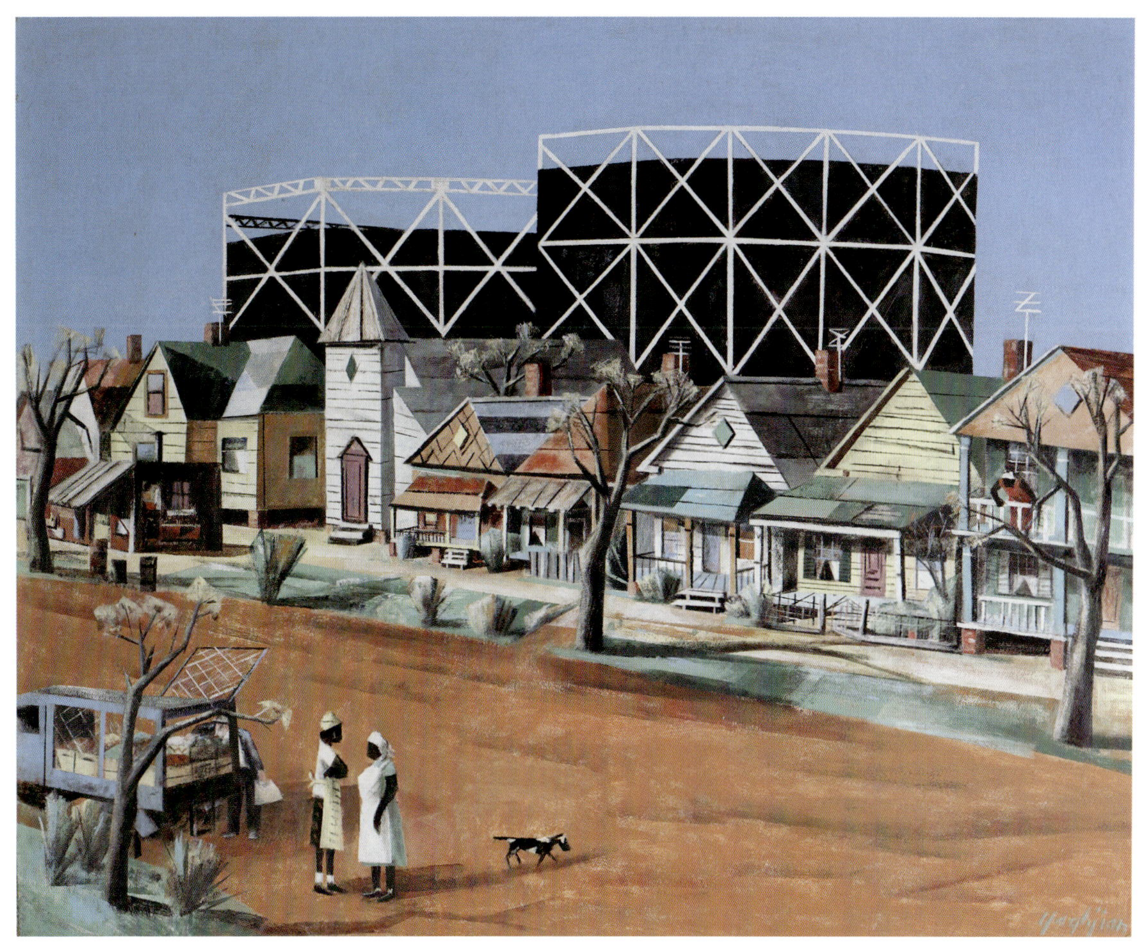

Morning on Huger Street, circa 1955 • Lacquer on board • 32 x 39 ½ • Greenville County Museum of Art, purchase from the Arthur and Holly Magill Fund

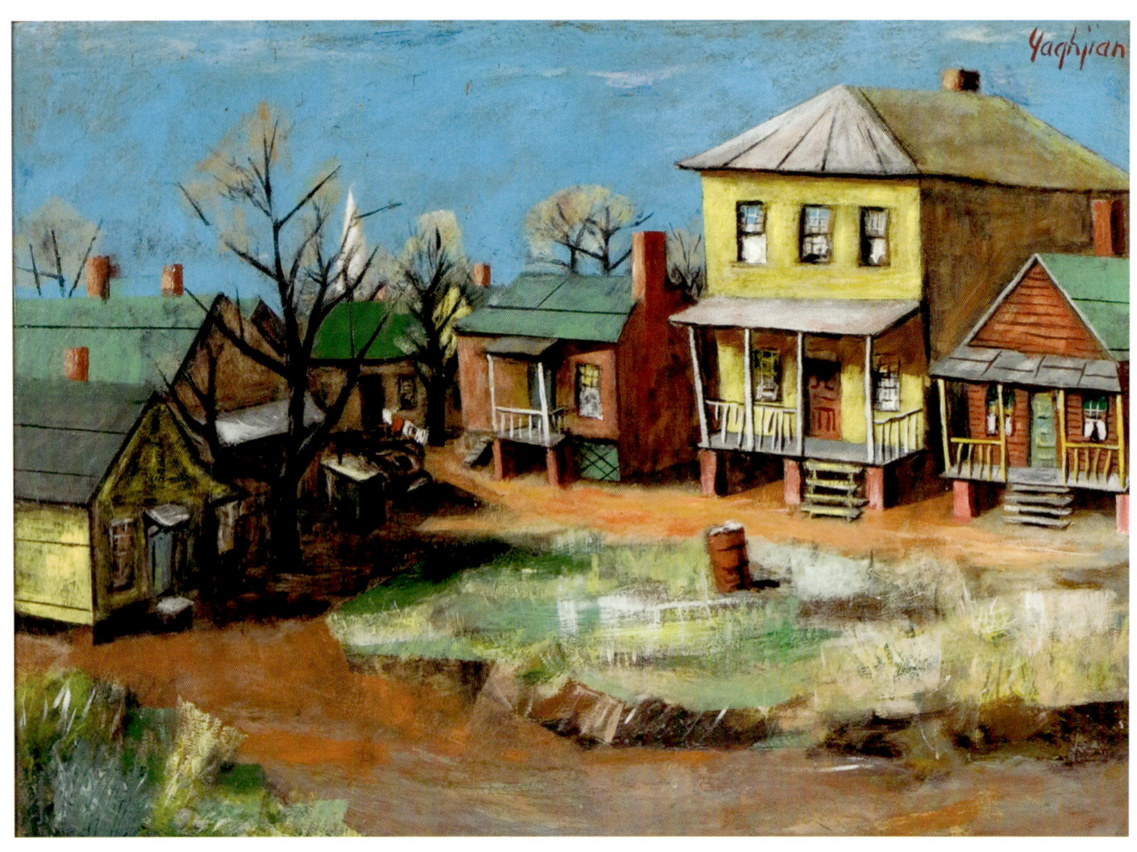

Around the Bend, circa 1950 • Lacquer on board • 20 x 28 • On loan from the Johnson Collection

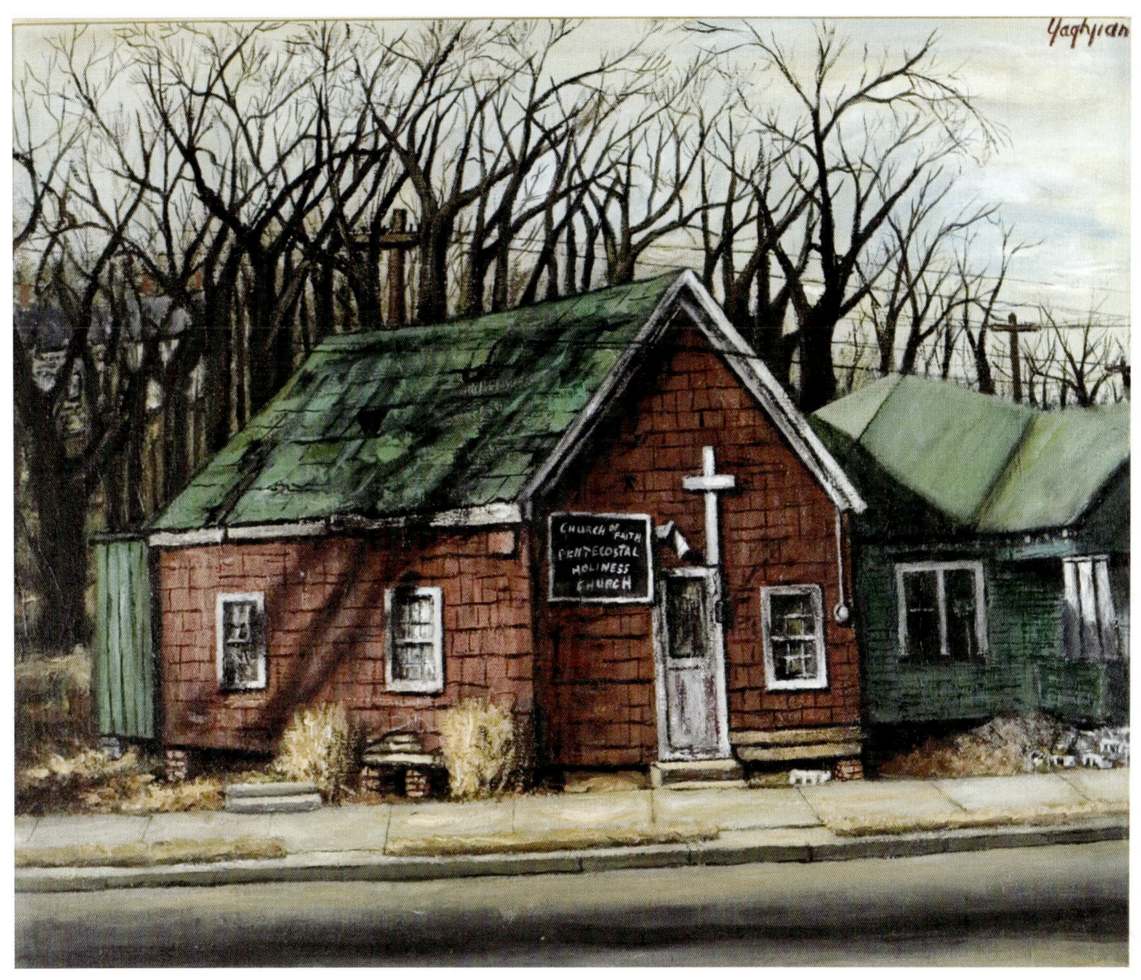

Pentecostal Holiness Church, circa 1960 • Acrylic on canvas • Size 29 x 35 • Collection of Ted and Karen Ramsaur

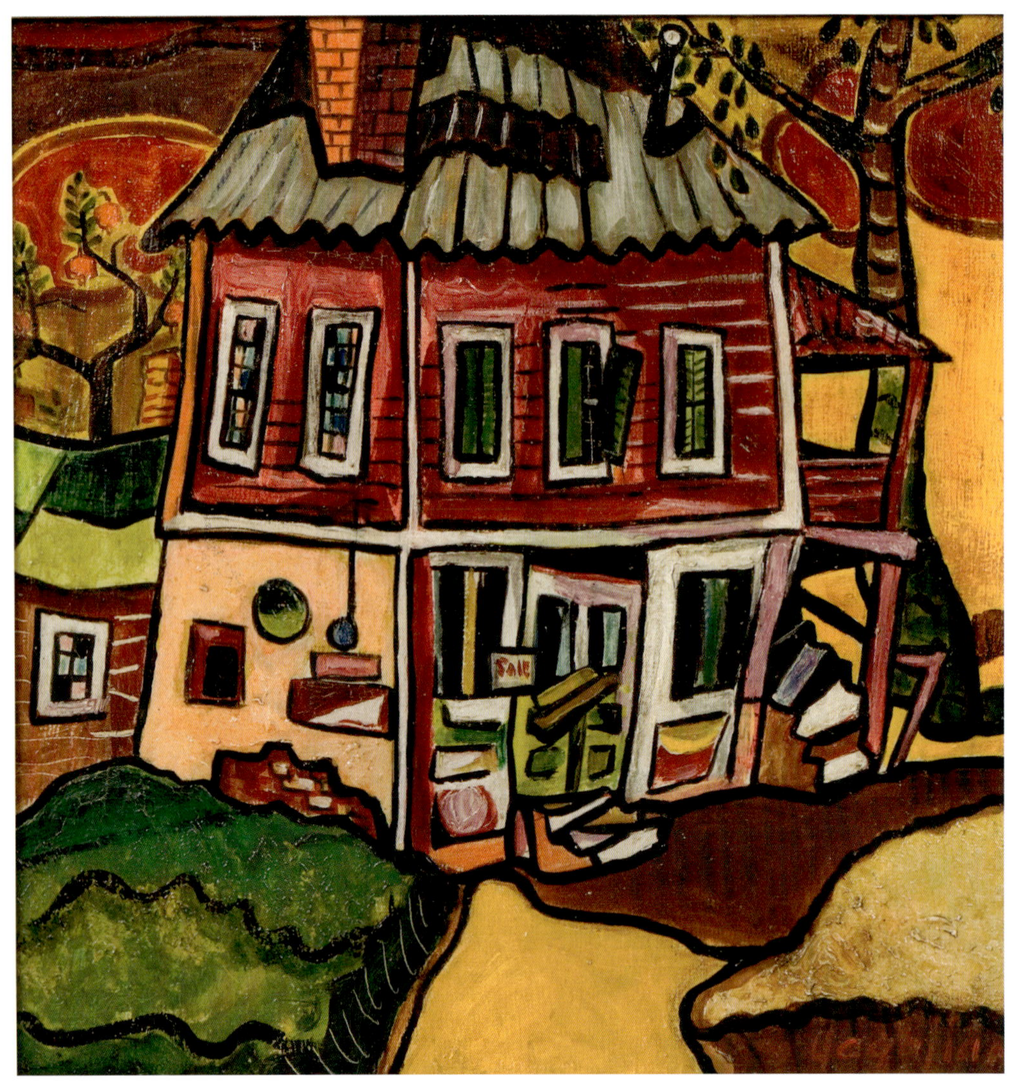

Corner House for Sale, 1950 • Oil on canvas • 15 x 15 • Collection of Candy Yaghjian Waites

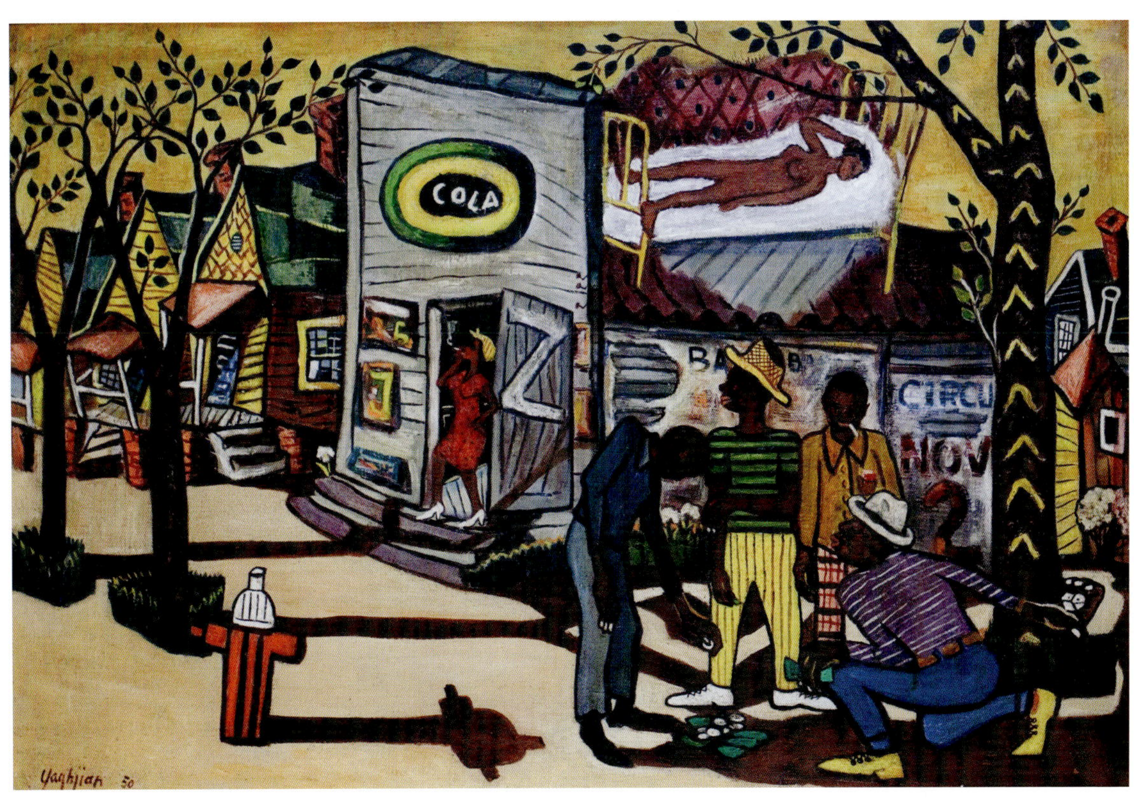

Doorway Distraction, 1950 • Oil on canvas • 24 x 36 • Collection of Candy Yaghjian Waites

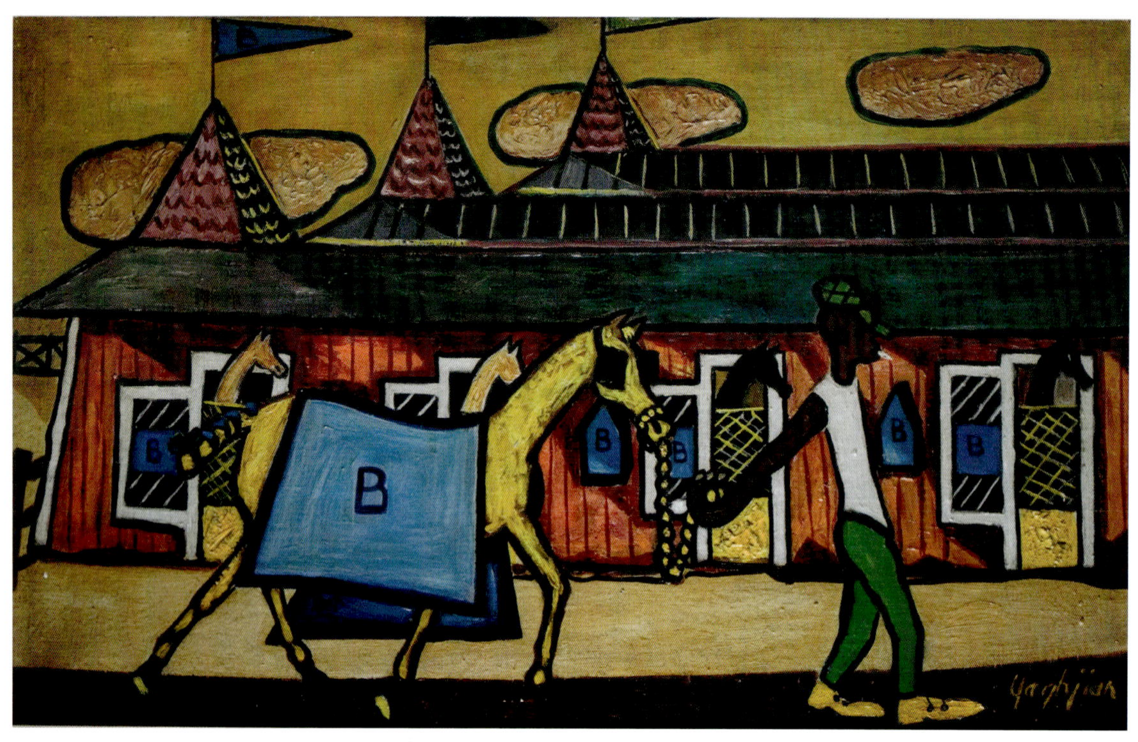

At B Stables, 1950 • Oil on canvas • 16 x 26 • Collection of David H. Yaghjian

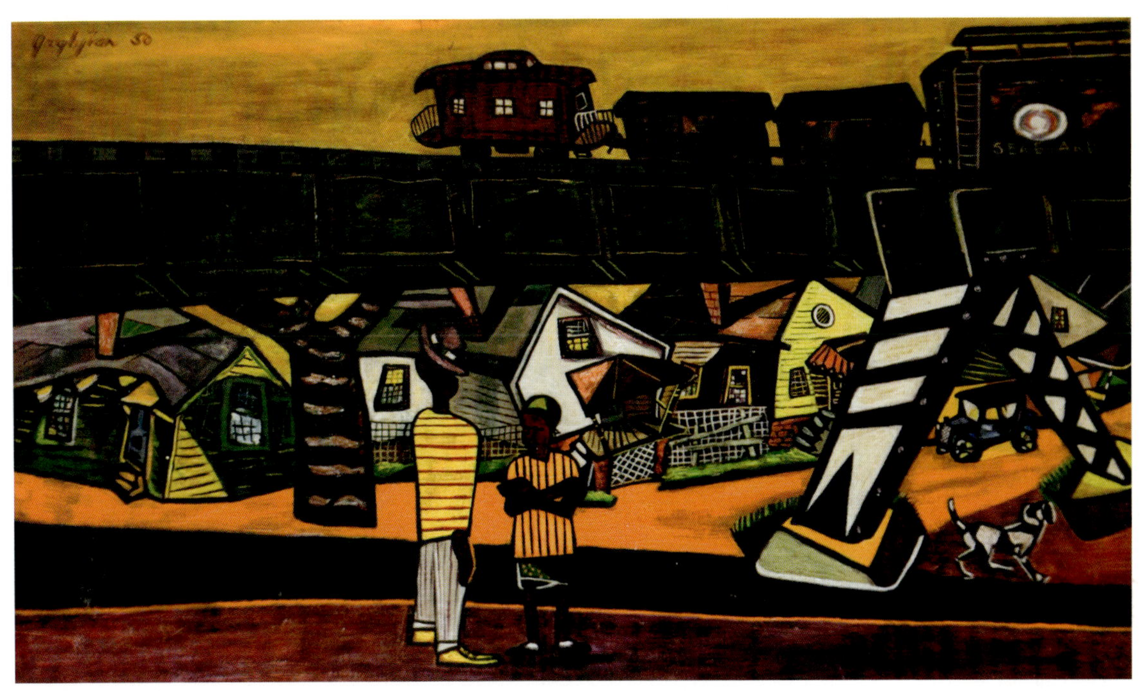

Red Caboose, Yellow Sky, 1950 • Oil on board • 20 x 34 • Collection of David H. Yaghjian

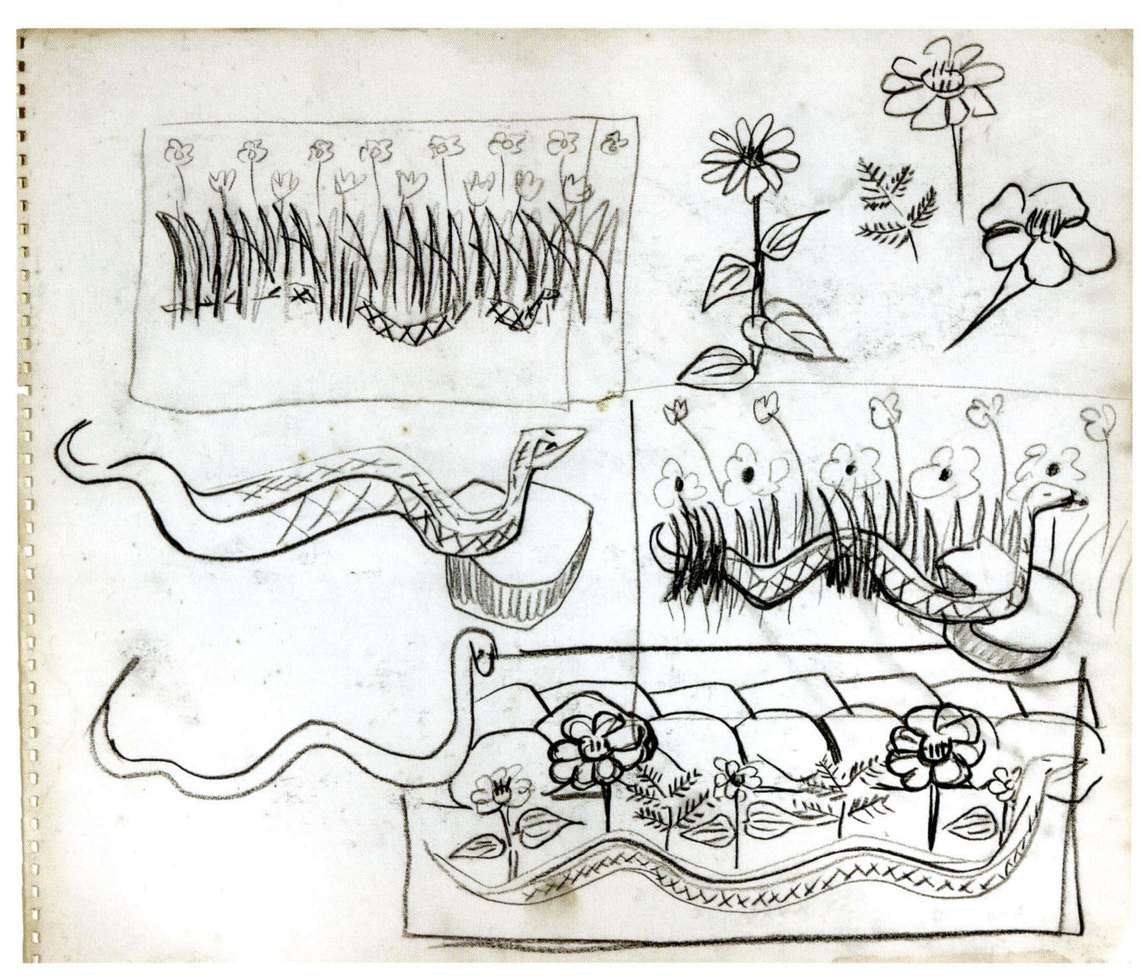

Untitled [Snake Sketch], circa 1949 • Graphite on paper • 14 x 17 • Private collection

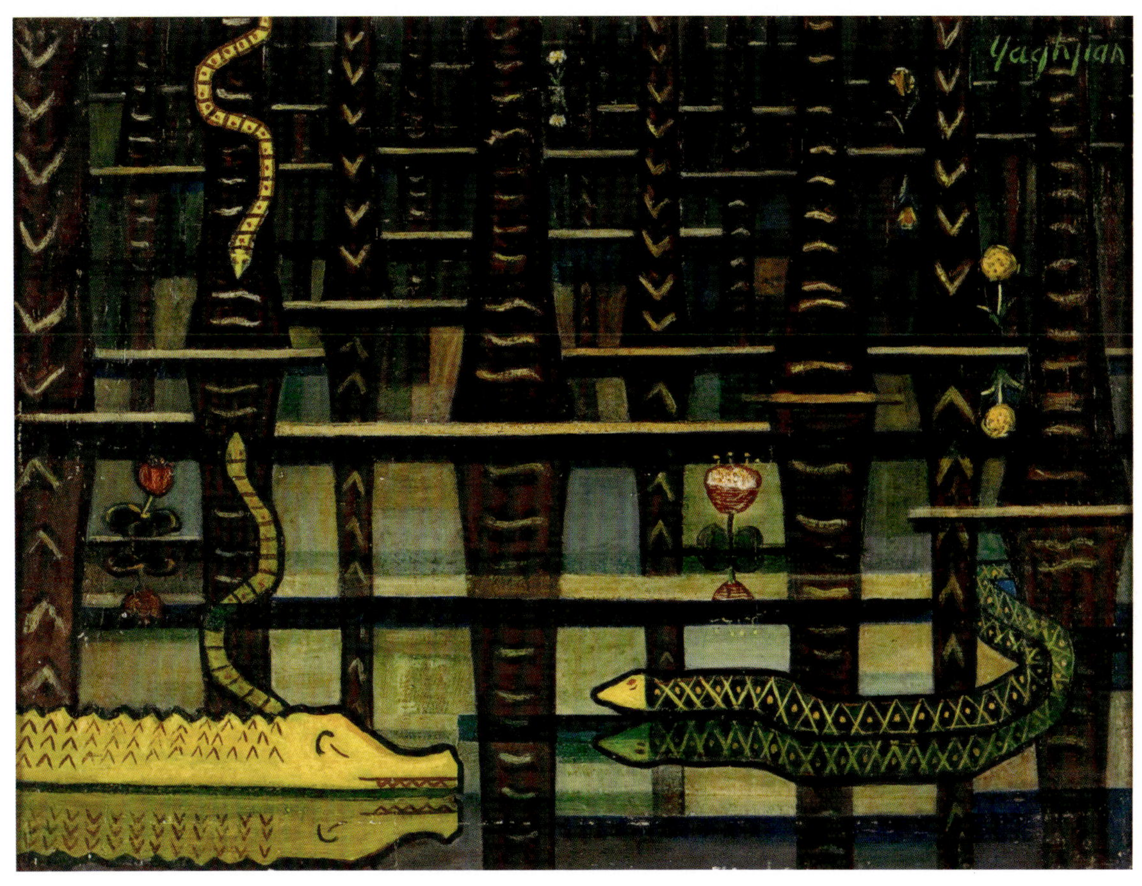

South Carolina Swamp, circa 1949 • Oil on canvas • 18 x 24 • Collection of David H. Yaghjian

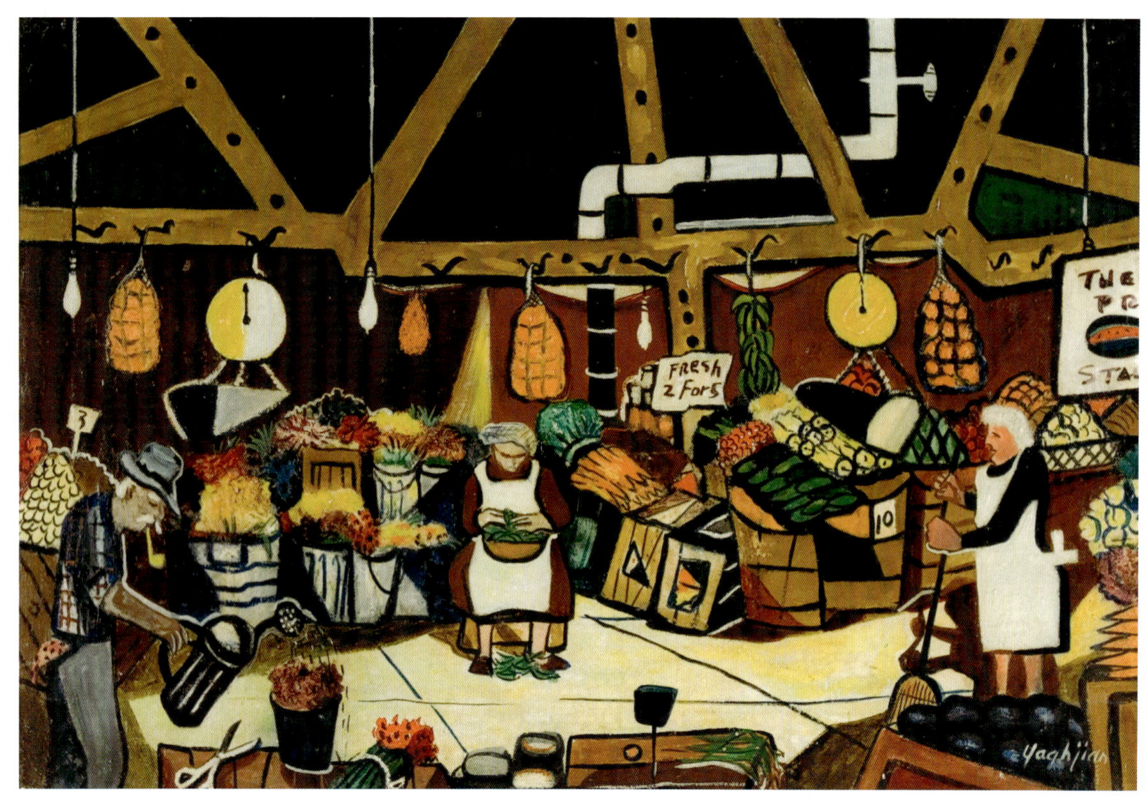

Assembly Street Market, circa 1950 • Oil on board • 20 x 30 • Private Collection

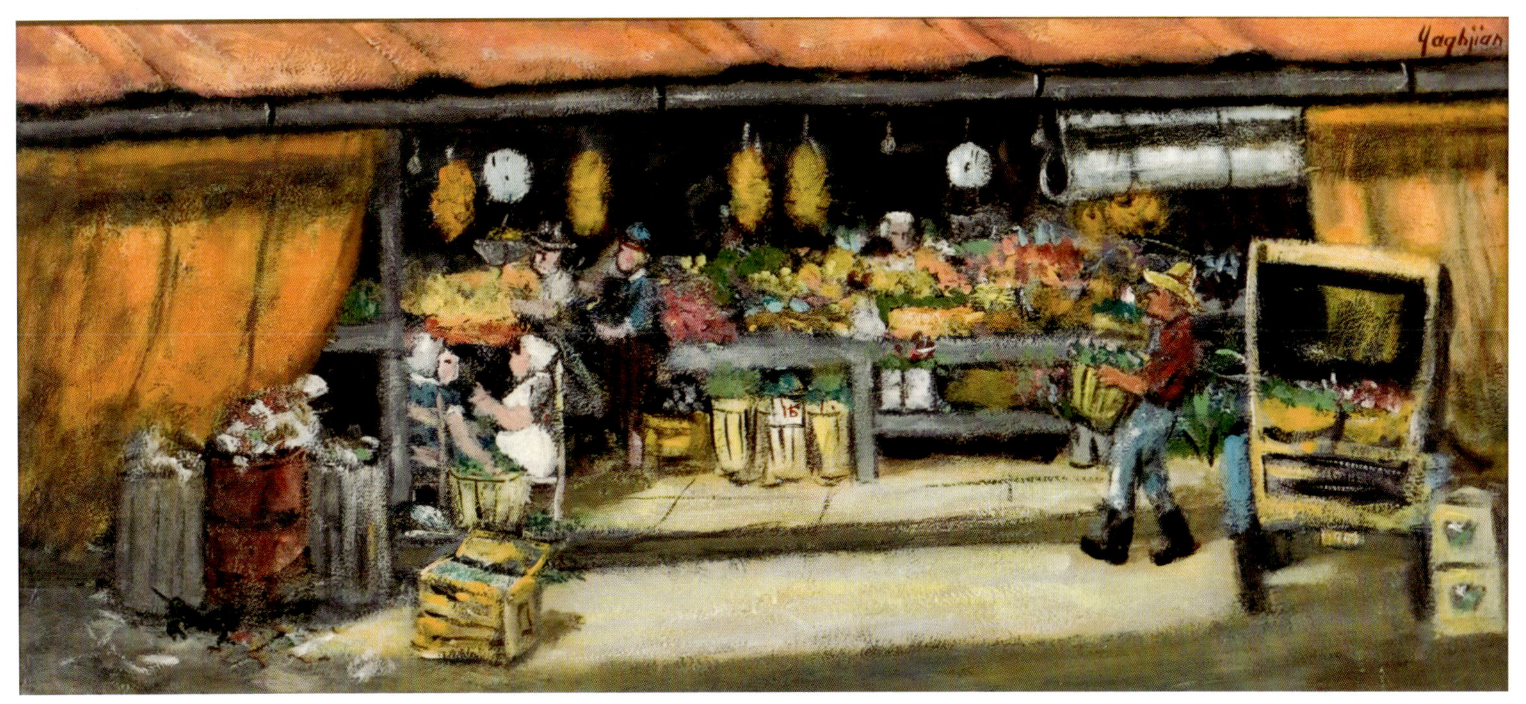

Bringing in Some Vegetables, circa 1965 • Lacquer on board • 18 x 40 • On loan from the Johnson Collection

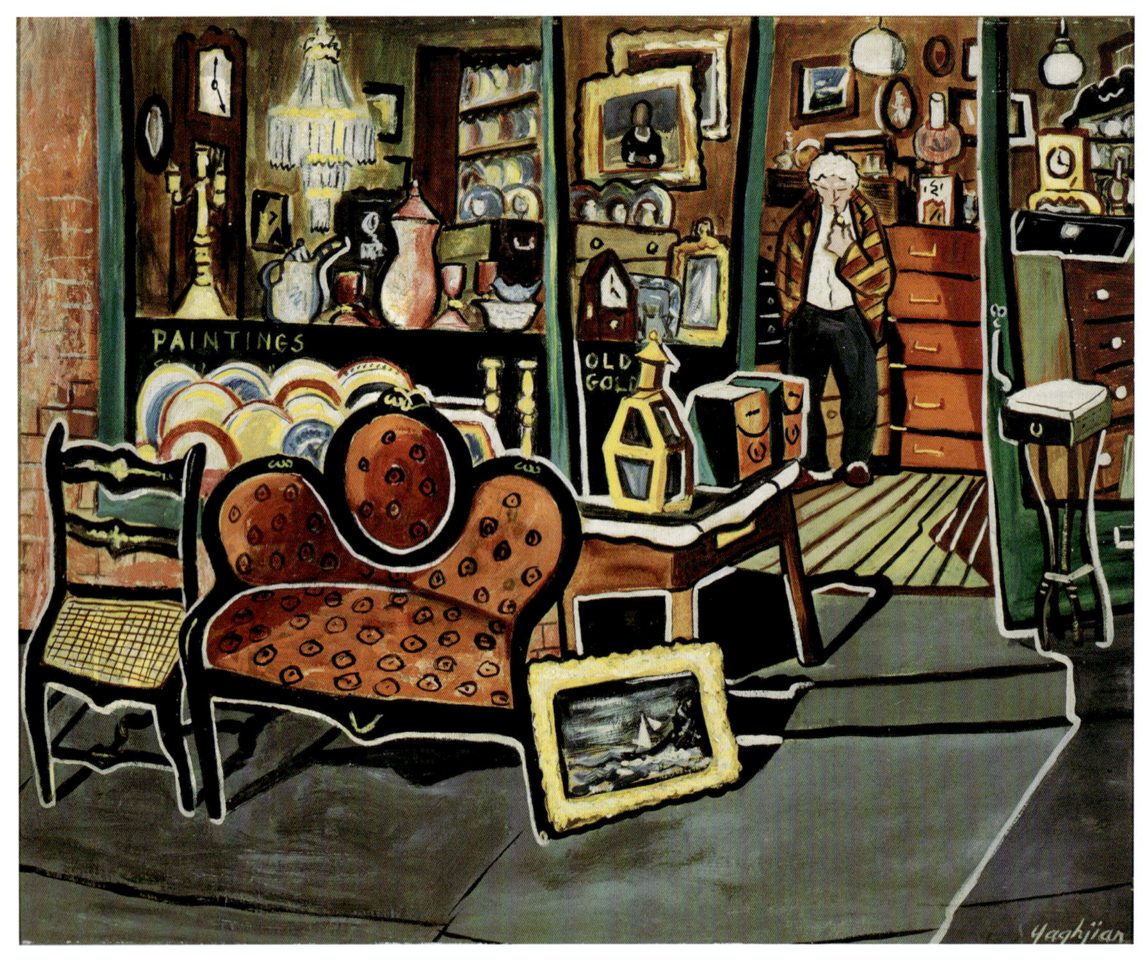

Gervais Street Antique Shop, circa 1950 • Oil on board • 22 ½ x 28 • Morris Museum of Art

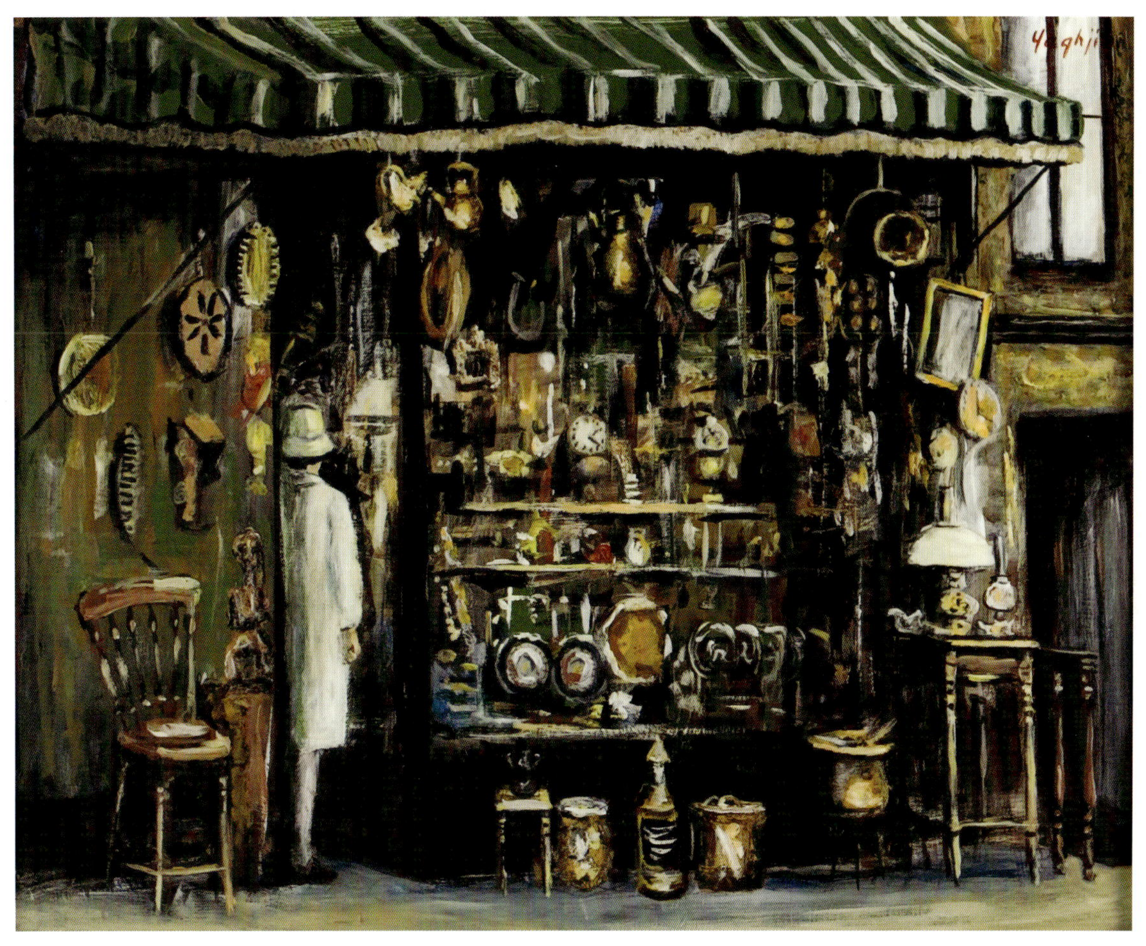

Untitled (Antique Shop), 1966 • Polymer on board • 24 x 30 • On Loan from the Estate of Jenny Clarkson Dreher

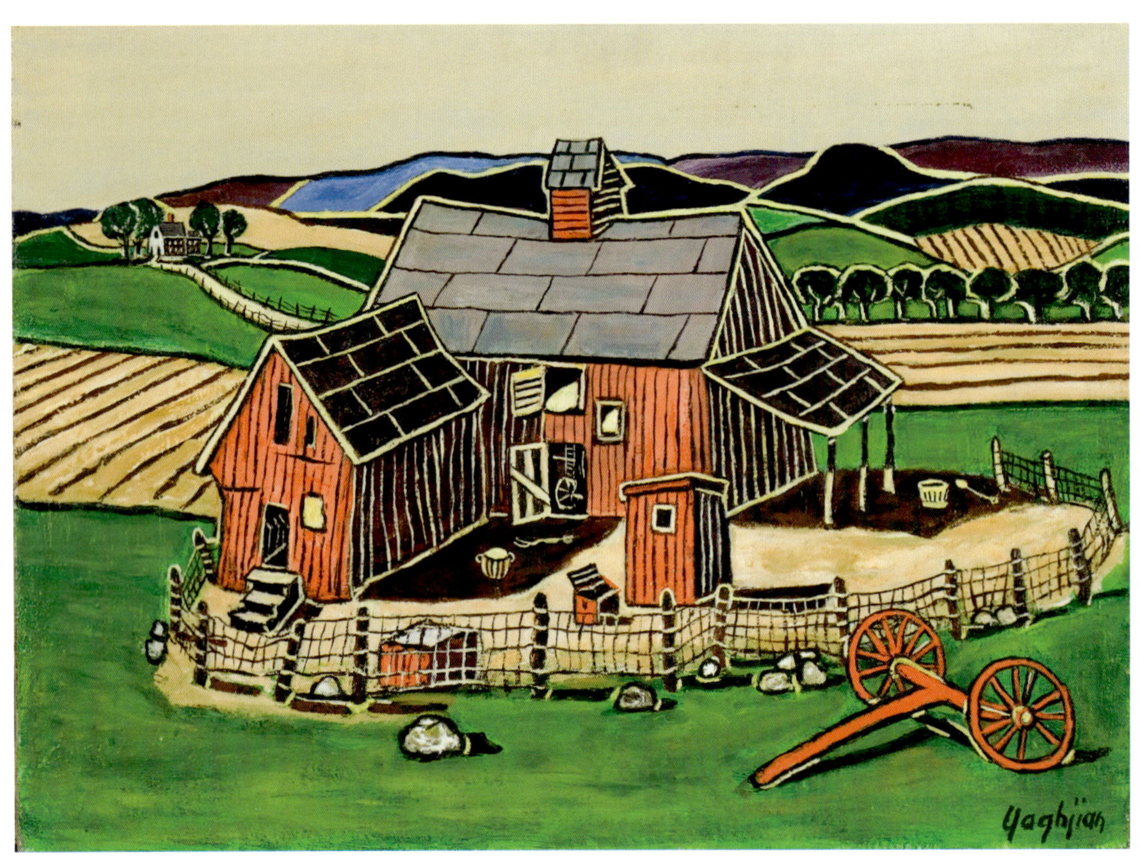

Old Barn in Danby, 1976 • Acrylic on canvas • 20 x 28 • Collection of Candy Yaghjian Waites

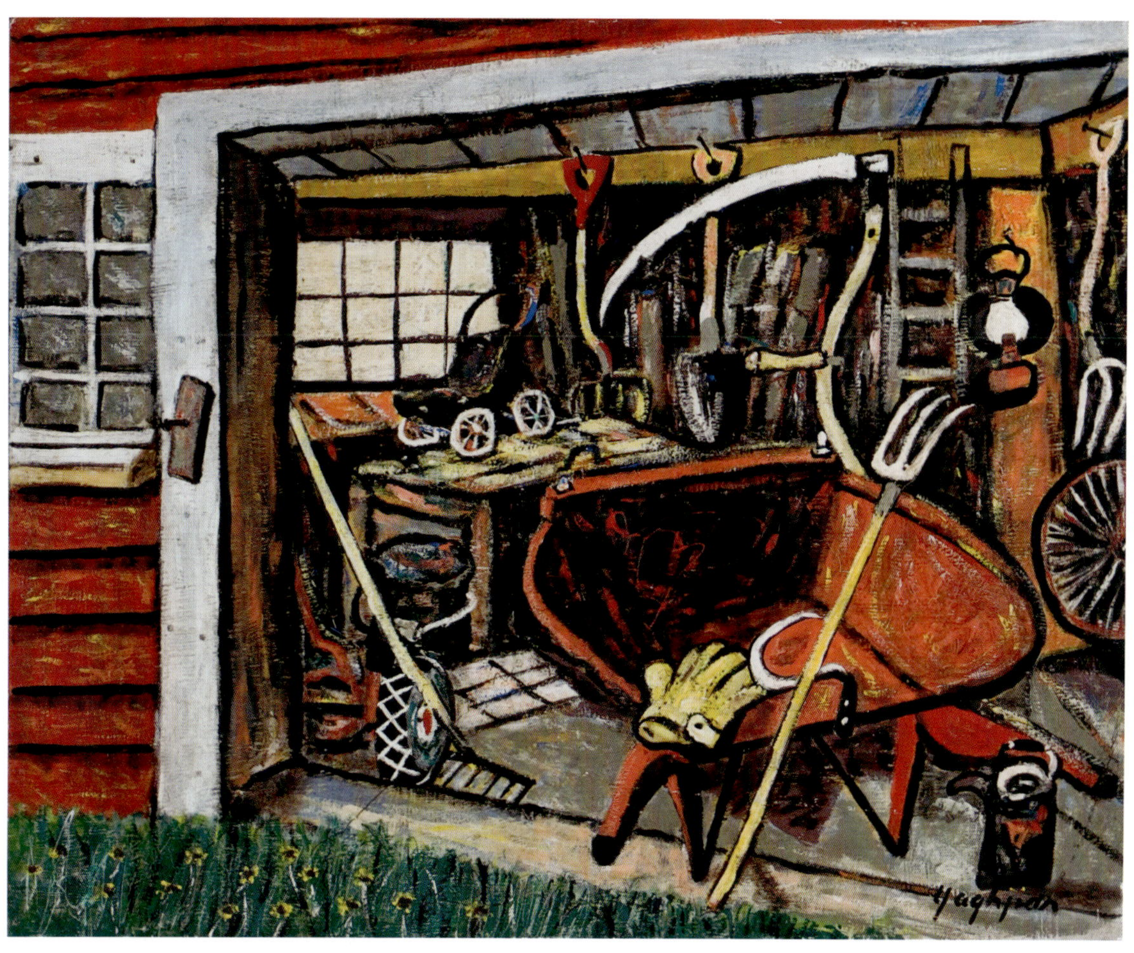

Lower Floor of Barn, 1953 • Lacquer on board • 24 x 30 • Collection of David H. Yaghjian

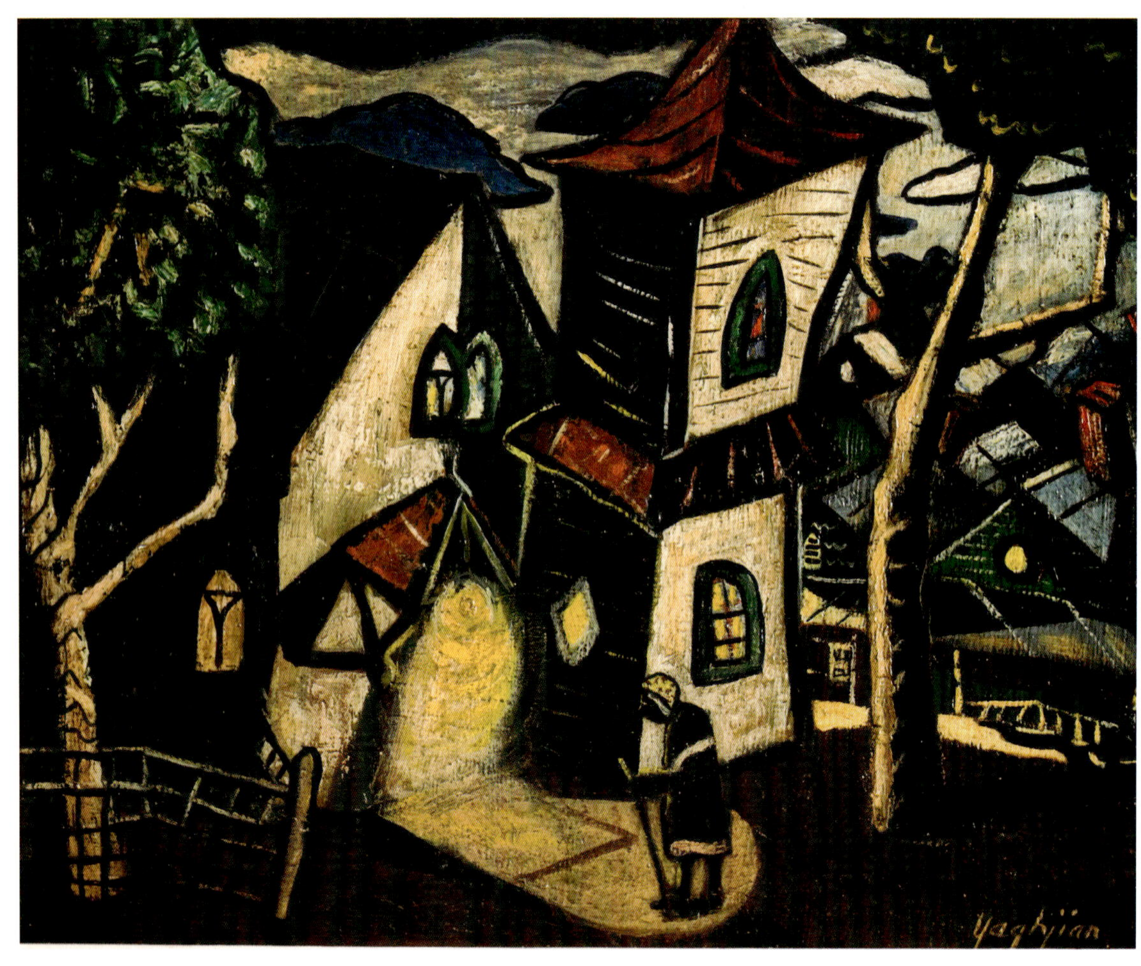

Evening Service, circa 1950 • Lacquer on board • 16 x 20 • Collection of Candy Yaghjian Waites

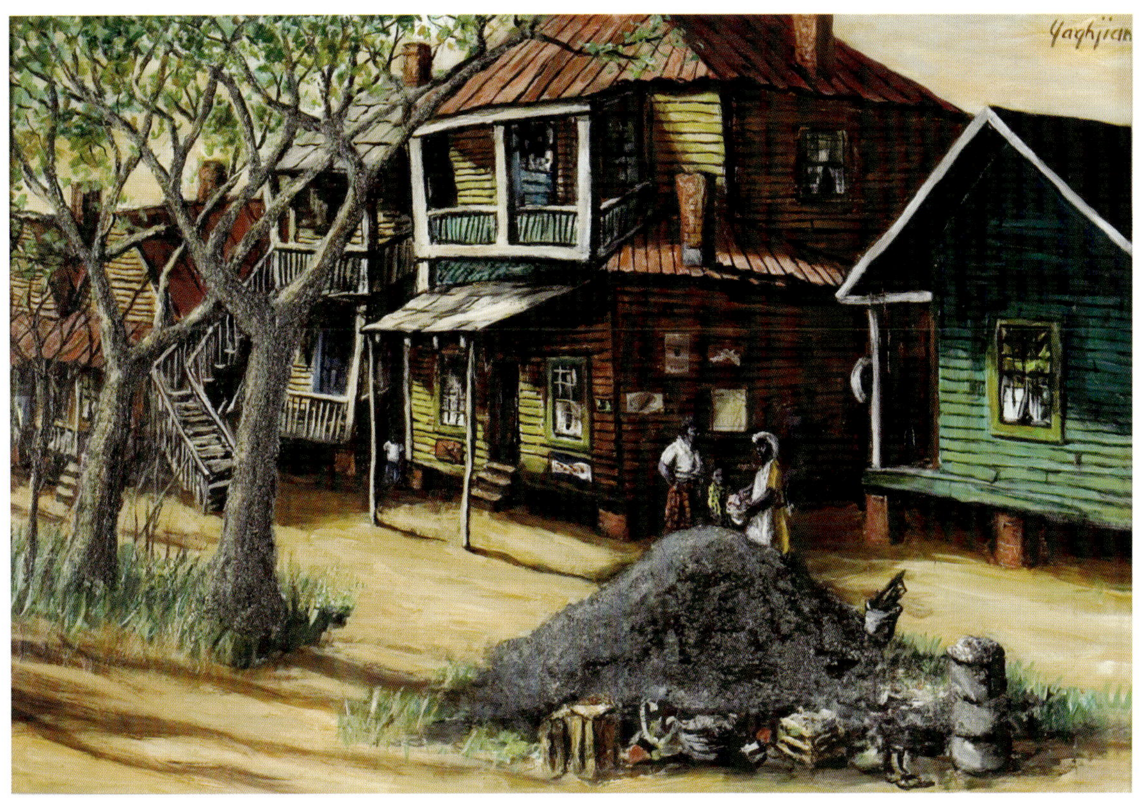

Dumping on Wheat Street, circa 1955 • Oil on board • 21 x 31 • Collection of Wade Cleveland

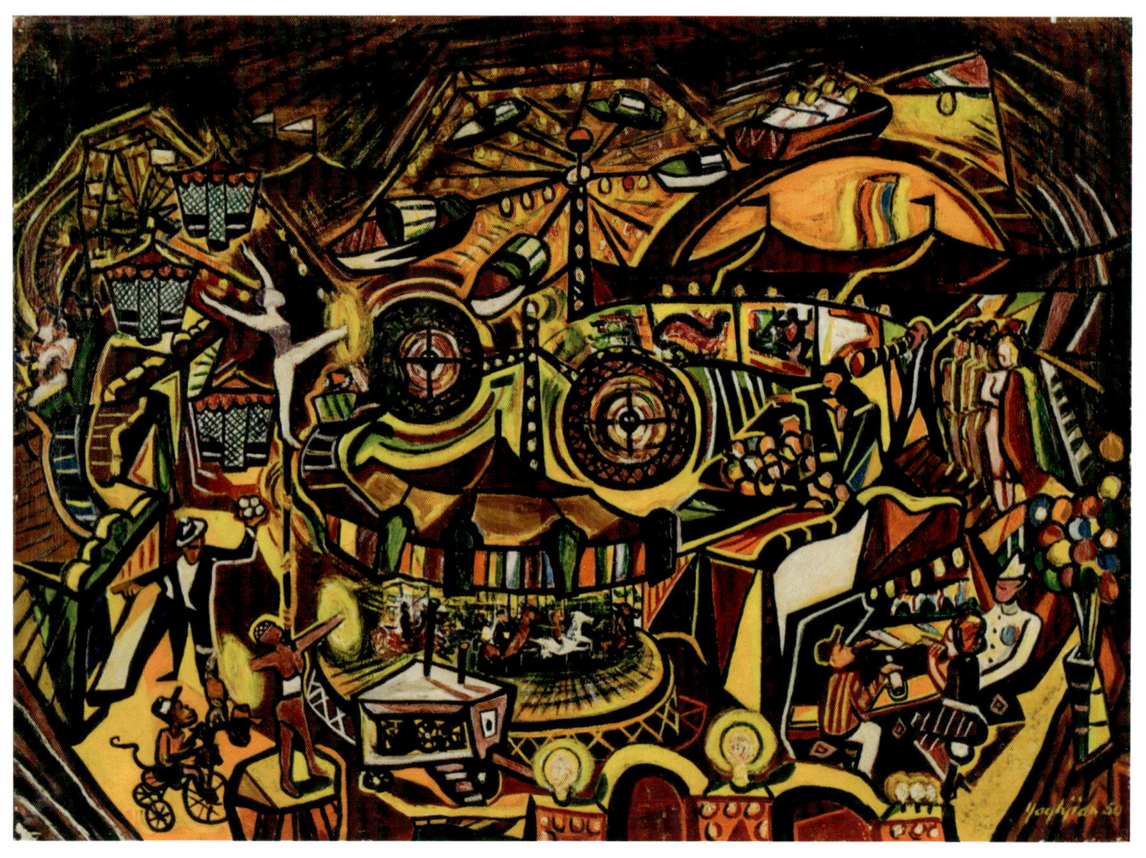

Columbia Fair, Hurry, Hurry, 1950 • Oil on canvas • 23 ½ x 32 • Collection of David H. Yaghjian

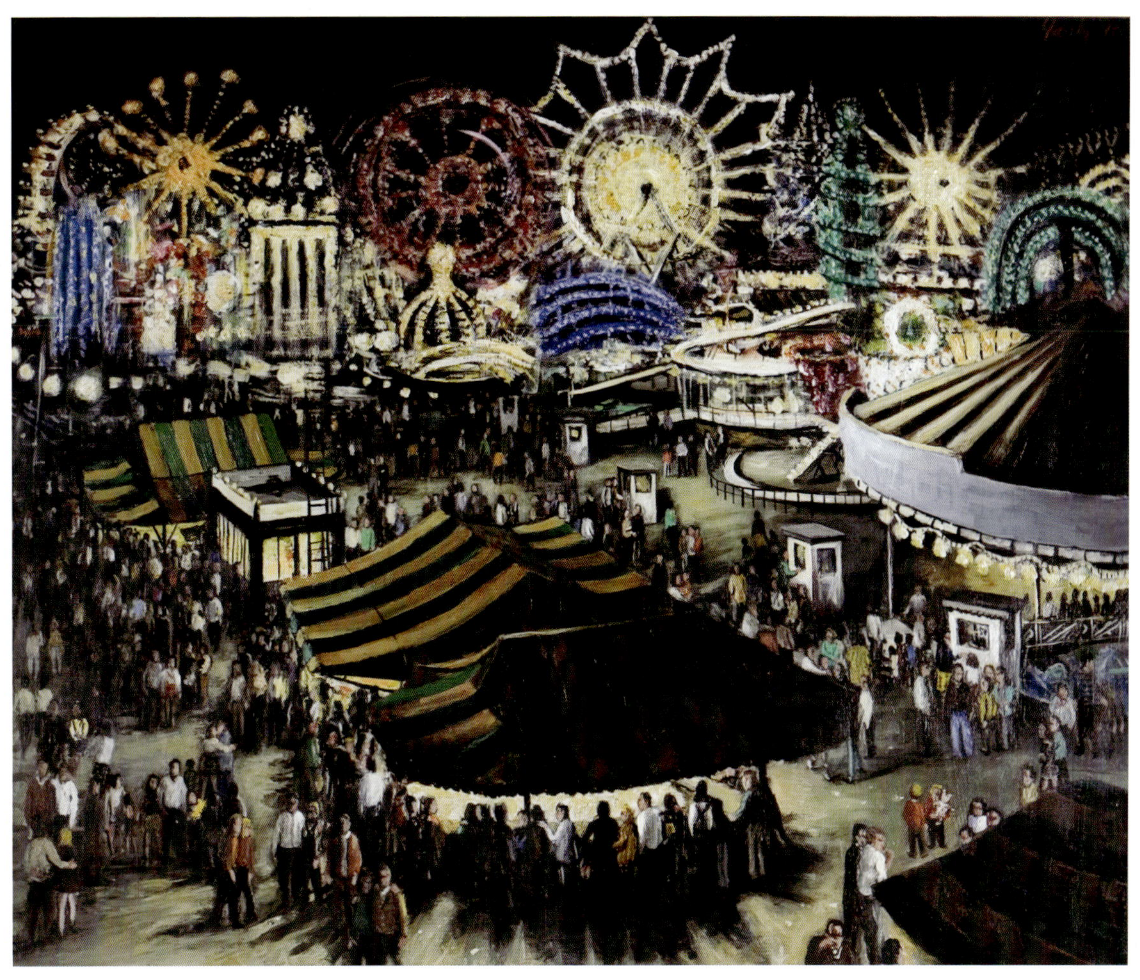

Night at the Fair, 1970 • Acrylic on board • 30 x 36 • South Carolina State Museum • Gift of Chuck Weldon

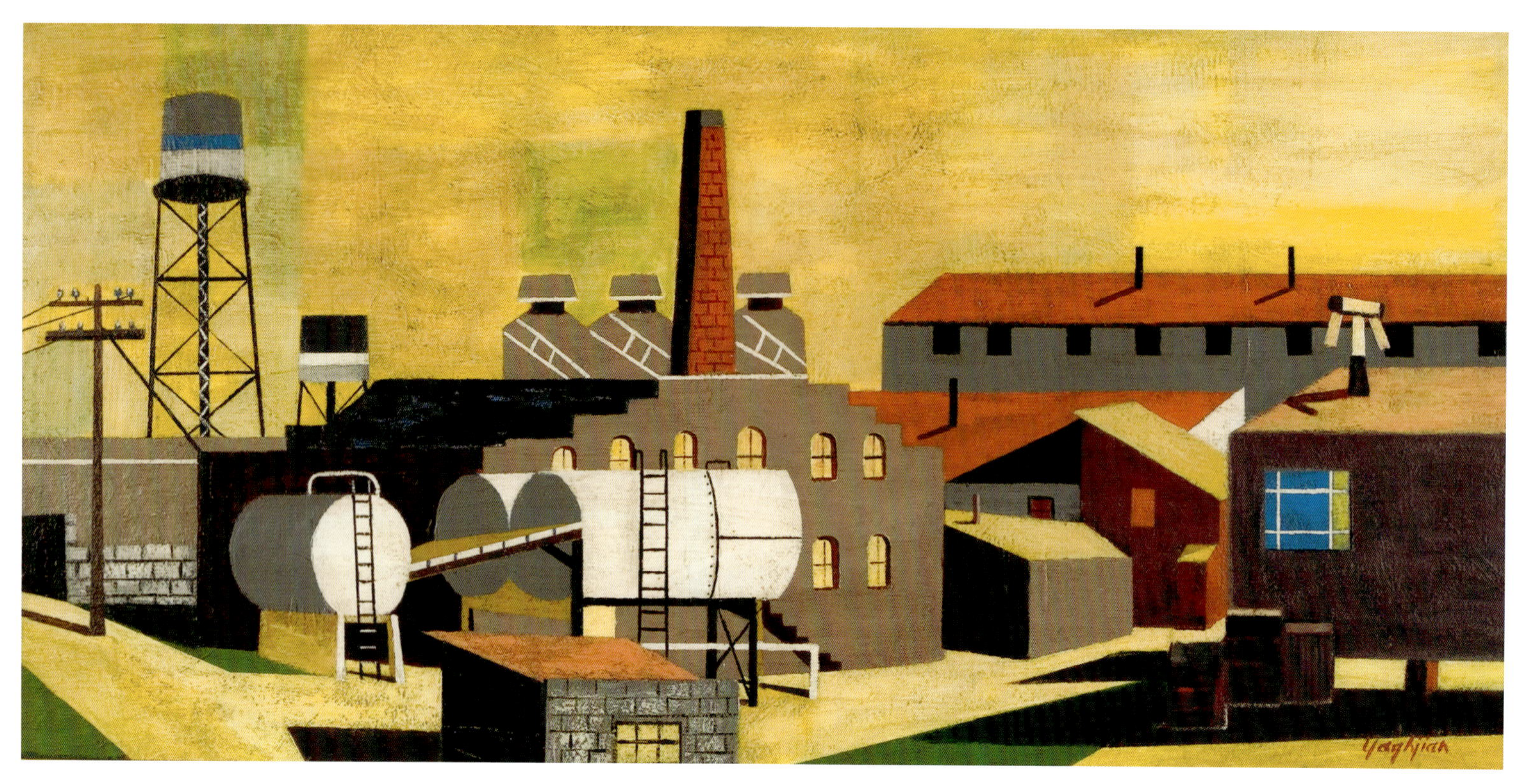

White Gas Tanks, circa 1955 • Lacquer on board • 17 ¾ x 35 ¾ • Collection of Wade Cleveland

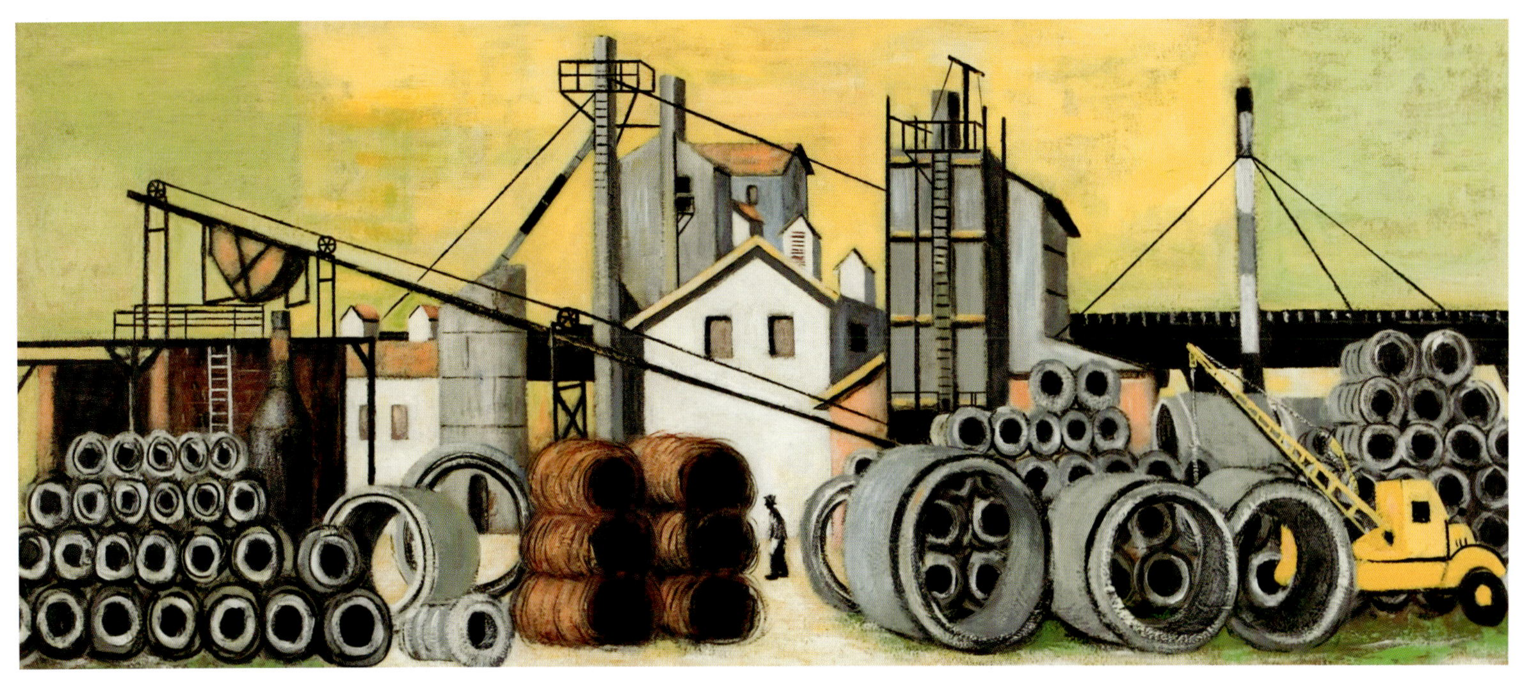

Concrete Works, circa 1955 • Lacquer on board • 17 x 39 • Collection of Tad and Maureen Mallory

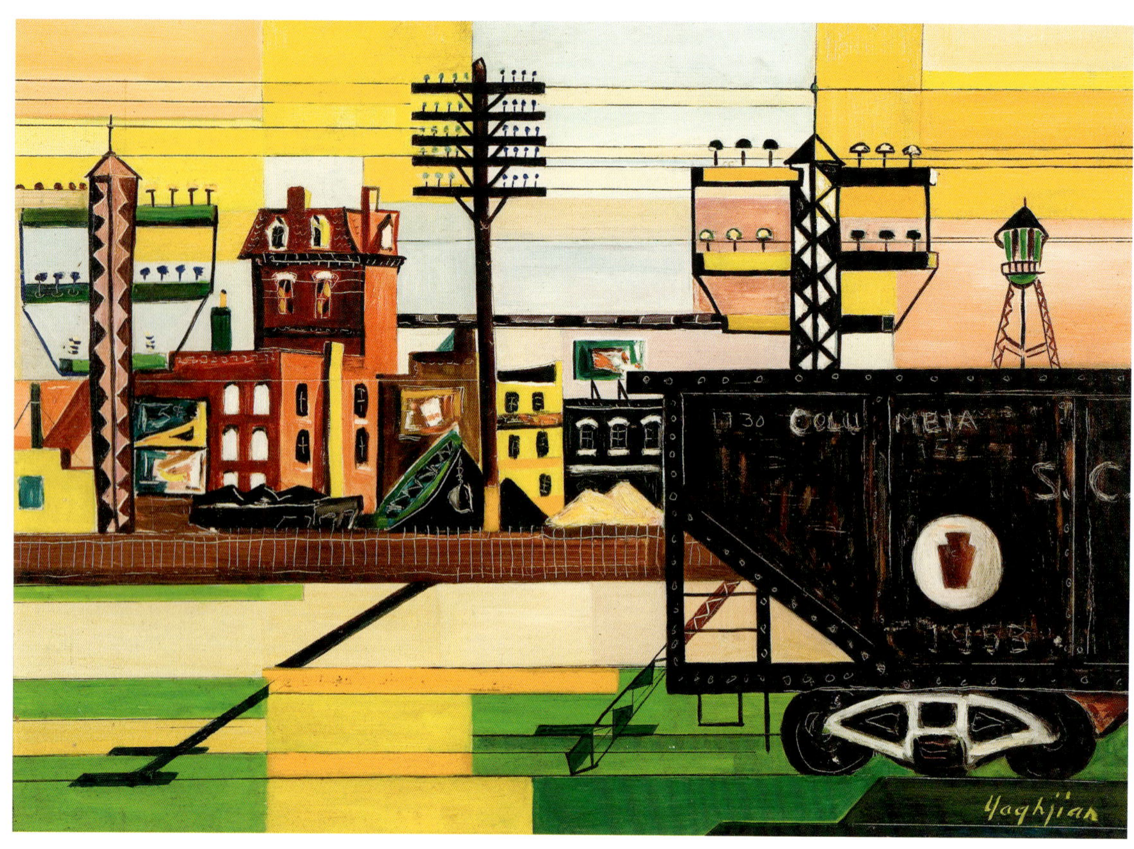

Coal Car, 1953 • Oil on board • 21 ¾ x 28 ½ • Columbia Museum of Art

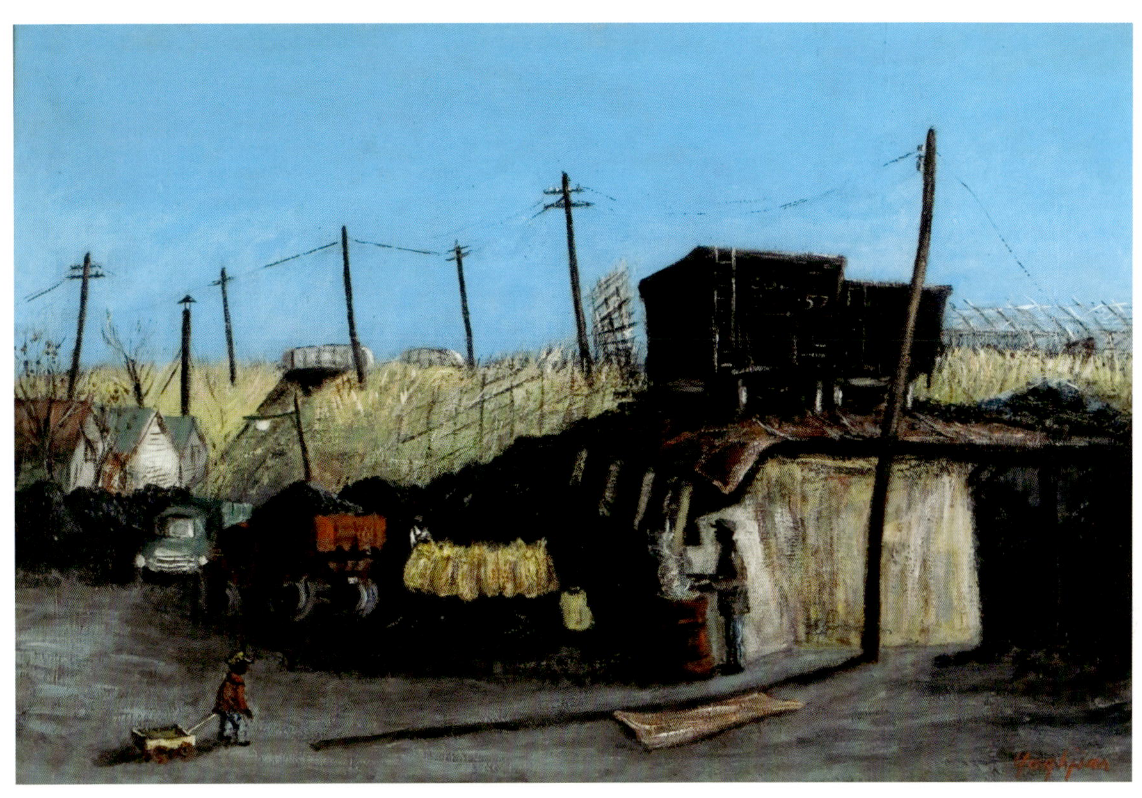

Coal Yard, 1957 • Lacquer on board • 24 x 36 • Collection of Carolina First

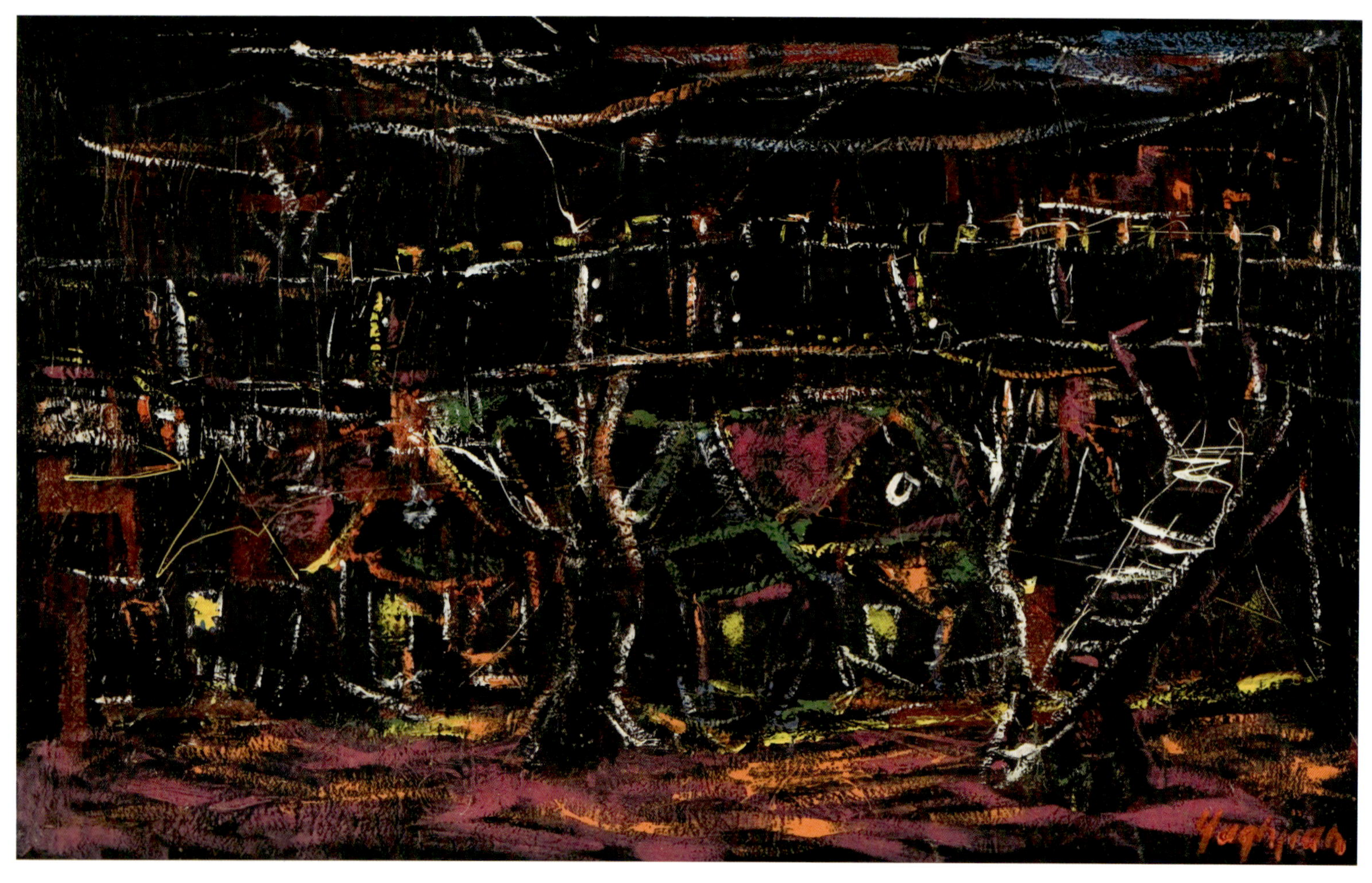

Night by the Tracks, circa 1960 • Lacquer on board • 16 x 26 • Collection of Candy Yaghjian Waites

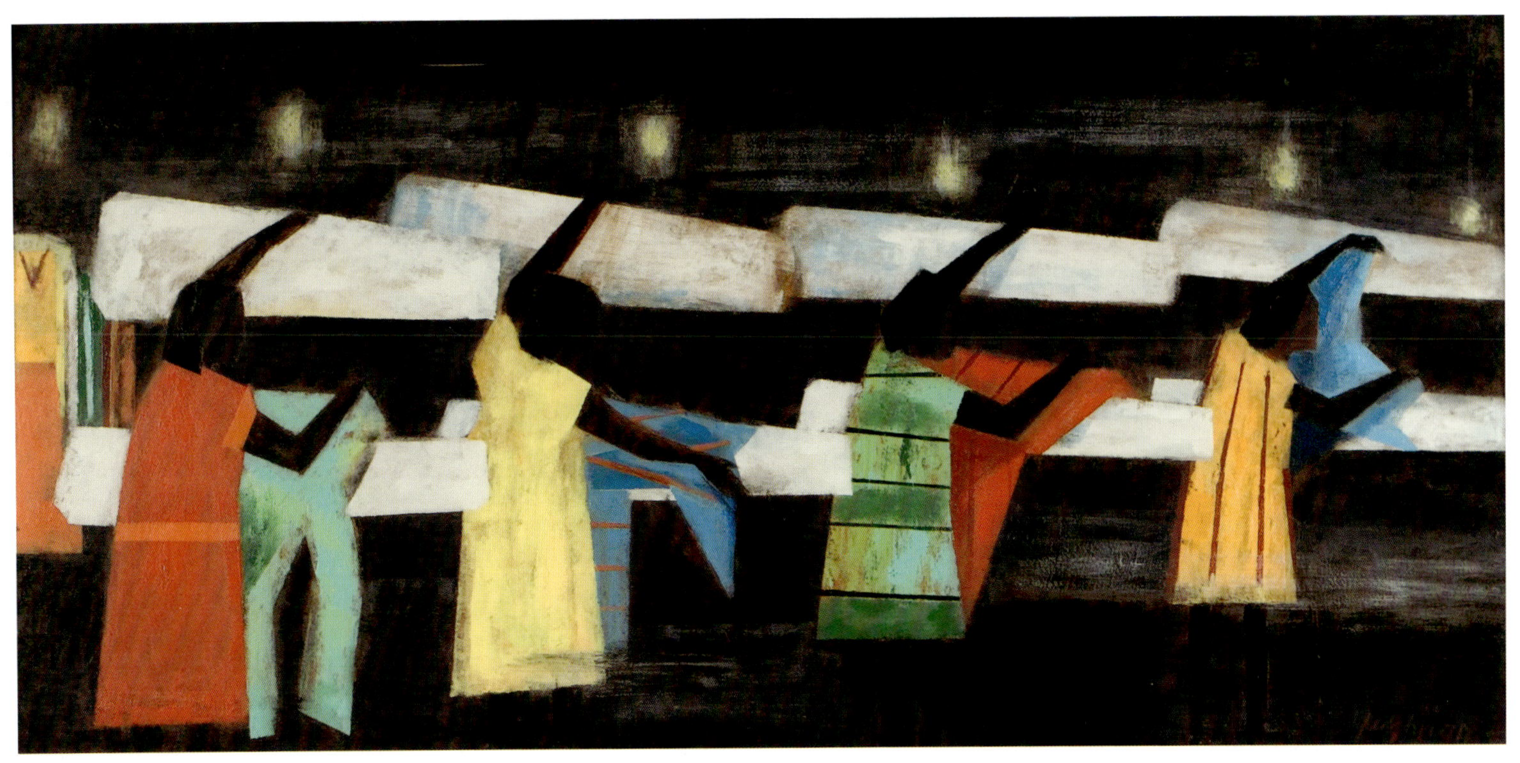

Master Cleaners, 1965 • Lacquer on board • 19 x 39 ½ • Courtesy of Clemson Advancement Foundation

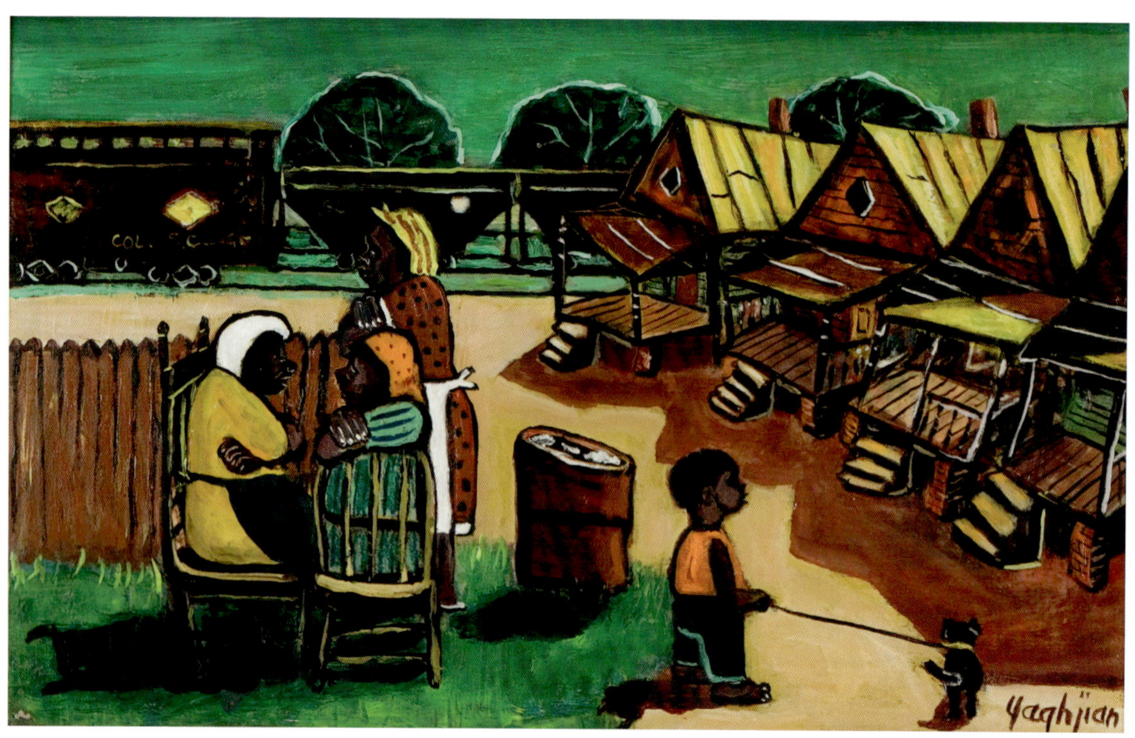

Break from House Work, circa 1975 • Acrylic on Board • 15 x 24 • On loan from the Steve and Darlene Coogler Collection, Greenville, SC

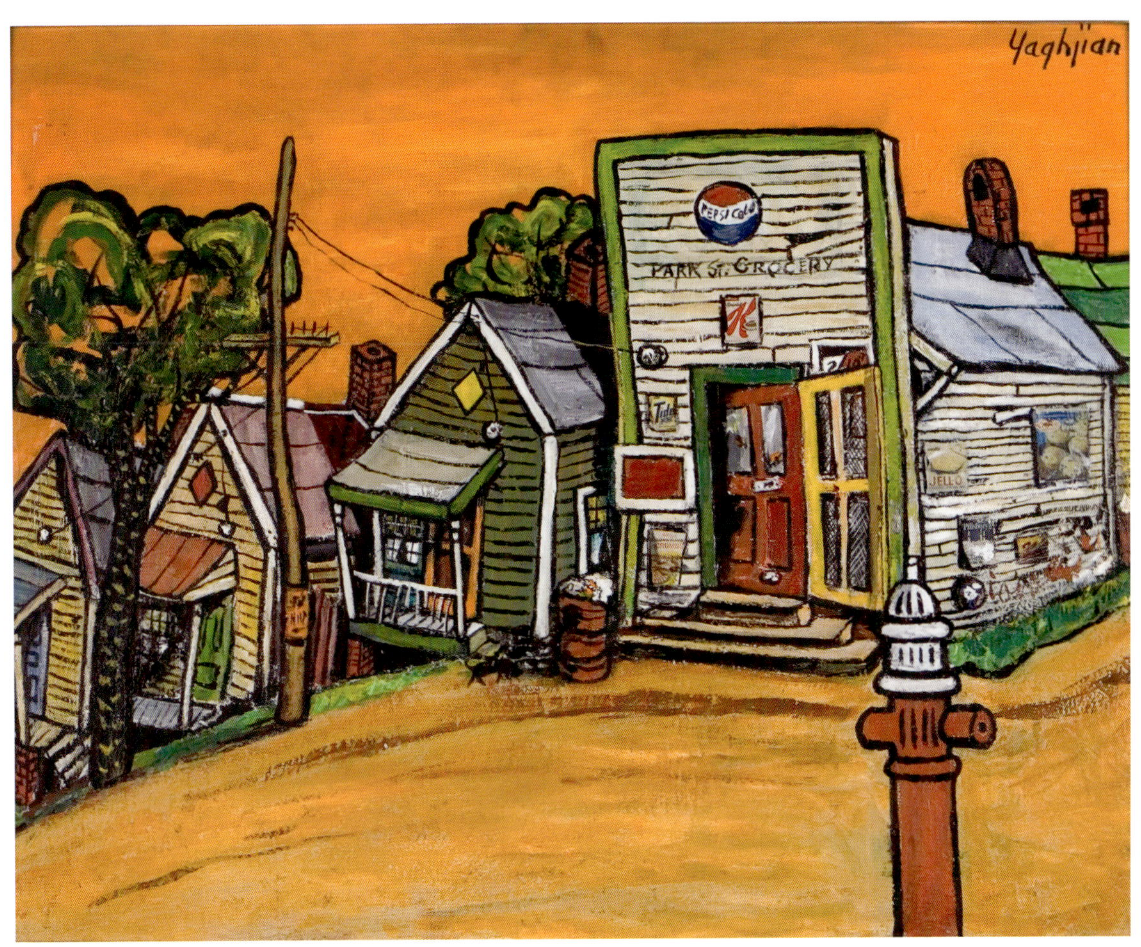

Park Street Grocery, circa 1975 • Acrylic on Canvas • 22 x 28 • On loan from the Johnson Collection

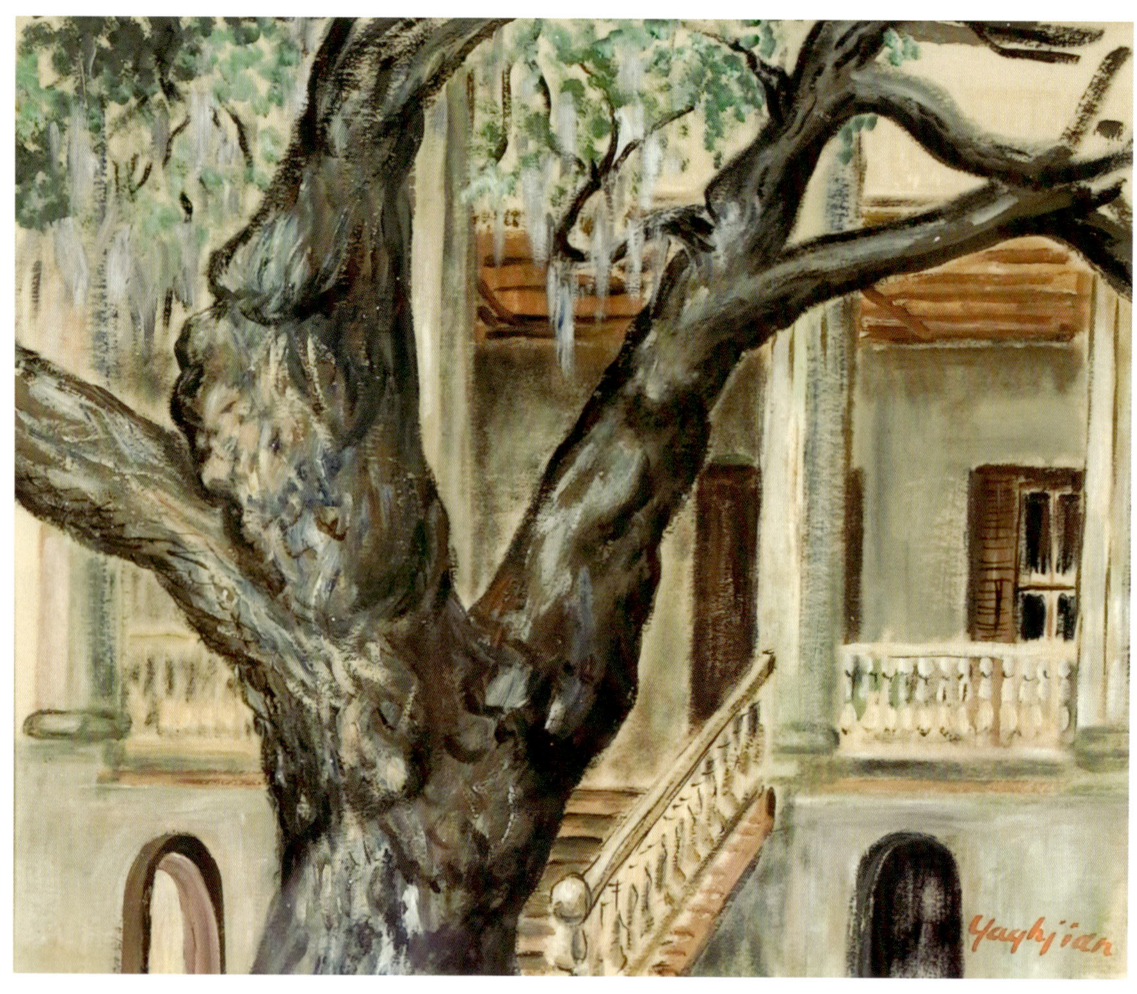

Charleston Scene, no date • Watercolor on paper• 14 x 16 ½ • Collection of the Bowie Art Center, Erskine College, Due West, SC

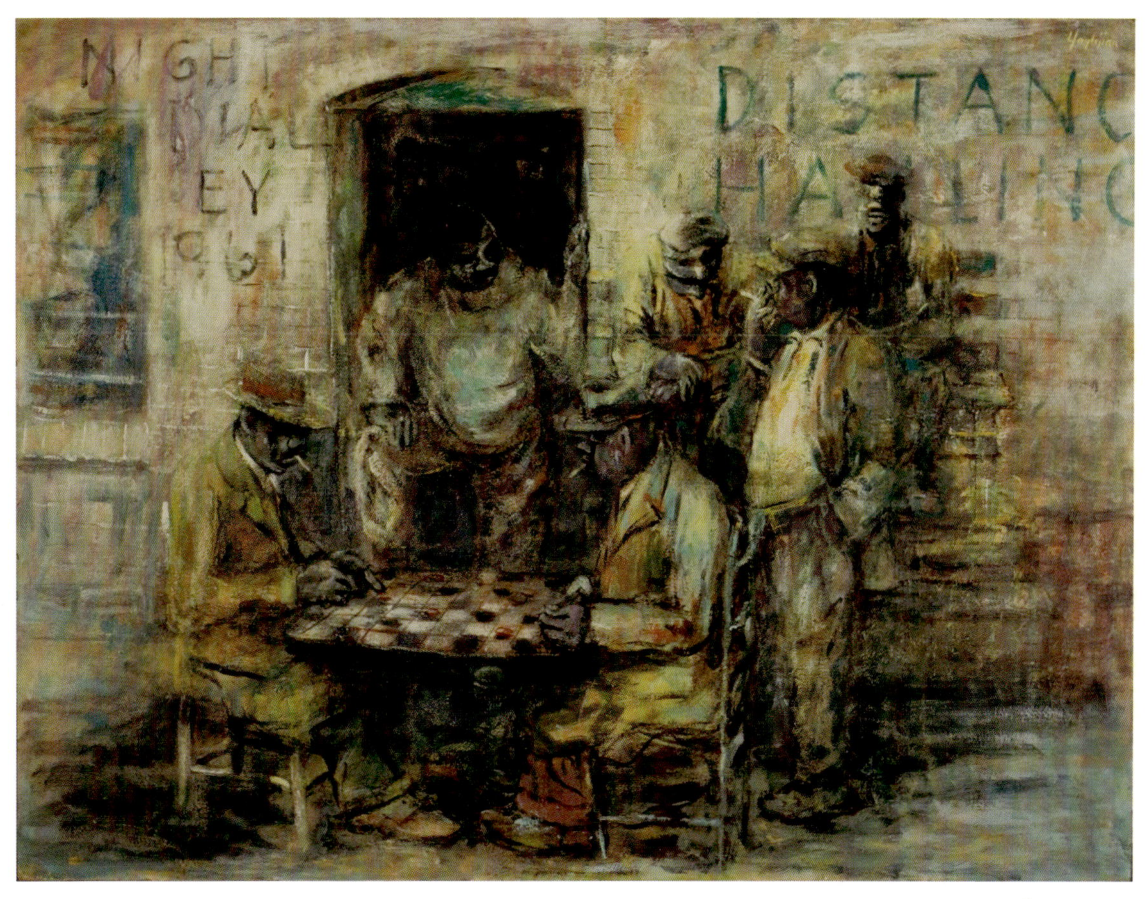

Waiting for Business, circa 1965 • Lacquer on board • 36 x 48 • Collection of David H. Yaghjian

Exhibition Checklist

Self Portrait, 1931
Oil on board
24 x 18
Collection of Susan A. Yaghjian

From My Studio on 10th Street, 1932
Oil on canvas
25 x 20
Collection of Candy Yaghjian Waites

Jersey Across Rooftops, 1933
Oil on board
22 x 18
Collection of David H. Yaghjian

57th Street from My Window, 1933
Oil on canvas
16 x 20
Collection of David H. Yaghjian

Columbus Circle, 1934
Oil on board
36 x 33
Collection of Candy Yaghjian Waites

42nd Street West of Broadway, 1934
Oil on canvas
42 x 36
Collection of Susan A. Yaghjian

Snow on 56th Street, 1934
Oil on canvas
16 x 20
Collection of David H. Yaghjian

Up the Hudson from Jersey, 1935
Oil on canvas
30 x 36
Collection of David H. Yaghjian

Up the Hudson from Jersey (Sketch),
circa 1935
Pencil on paper
9 x 12
Private Collection

Across to Jersey, 1935
Oil on board
14 x 17
collection of Candy Yaghjian Waites

Most Any Night on Columbus Circle,
1935
Oil on canvas
24 x 38
On loan from the Estate of Dorothy
Candy Yaghjian

Goldman's Band in Central Park, 1935
Oil on canvas
24 x 38
Collection of David H. Yaghjian

Times Square, circa 1935
Oil on canvas
36 x 40
On loan from the Estate of Dorothy
Candy Yaghjian

Looking for Work in the 1930's
Pencil on paper
12 x 8 ¾
Private Collection

Snow on the Rooftops, circa 1935
Oil on canvas
30 x 36
On loan from the Estate of Dorothy
Candy Yaghjian

Manhattan from the Bowery, circa
1935
Oil on canvas
30 x 36
Collection of Candy Yaghjian Waites

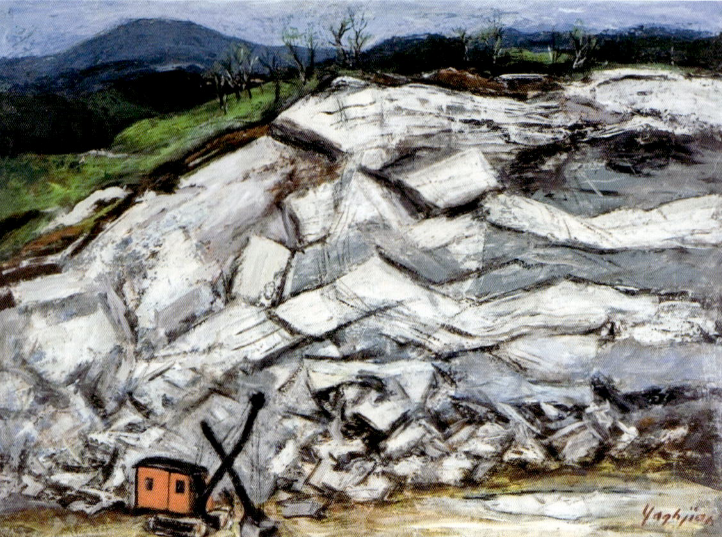
Quarry Near Danby, c. 1955

Night in Manhattan, 1936
Oil on board
24 x 36
On loan from the Estate of Dorothy
Candy Yaghjian

Bridges on the East River, 1936
Oil on canvas
20 x 25
Collection of David H. Yaghjian

Untitled Sketch [Against WPA Cuts],
circa 1936
Pencil on paper
10 ¾ x 8
Private Collection

Summer Night in Central Park, 1936
Oil on canvas
20 x 30
Collection of David H. Yaghjian

The White Church, 1936
Oil on canvas
26 7/16 x 32 7/16
On loan from the Smithsonian
American Art Museum, Transfer
from the Internal Revenue Service
through the General Services
Administration

Newsstand on 57th Street, circa 1937
Oil on canvas
16 x 20
Collection of David H. Yaghjian

Tugboats on the East River, 1937
Oil on canvas
24 x 36
Collection of Candy Yaghjian Waites

Looking Down the Hudson, 1937
Oil on canvas
16 x 24
Collection of Susan A Yaghjian

Jitterbugging on the Mall, 1938
Oil on canvas
22 x 28
Private Collection

El Crossing at 53rd Street, 1938
Oil on canvas
30 x 36
Collection of Susan A. Yaghjian

Lower Manhattan in the Late 1930's
Oil on board
30 x 36
On loan from the Johnson Collection

Playing Poker in My Studio, circa 1938
Oil on canvas
25 x 30
Collection of David H. Yaghjian

Subway at 57th Street, 1939
Oil on canvas
24 x 30
Collection of Susan A. Yaghjian

8th Avenue El, 1940
Oil on canvas
16 x 20
Collection of David H. Yaghjian

Untitled (Ossining, New York), 1943
Watercolor on paper
16 ½ x 21 ¾
Private Collection

Red Store in Ossining, New York, 1943
Watercolor on paper
11 ½ x 16 ¼
Private Collection

Coal Cars in Ossining, New York, 1943
Watercolor on paper
15 ½ x 22 ¾
Private Collection

Junk Yard in Ossining, New York, 1943
Watercolor on paper
15 ¼ x 21
Private Collection

Junk Yard with Wrecker in Ossining, New York, 1943
Watercolor on paper
15 ½ x 22 ½
Private Collection

Oil Tanks in Ossining, New York, 1943
Watercolor on paper
15 ¾ x 22
Private Collection

Docks in Ossining, New York, 1943
Watercolor on paper
15 ¼ x 19 ½
Private Collection

Candy and Mother Waiting for the Mail, 1944
Oil on canvas
25 x 33
Collection of Candy Yaghjian Waites

Ossining, 1944
Oil on canvas
20 x 30
Collection of Susan A. Yaghjian

Sunday Papers, 1944
Oil on canvas
24 x 18
Collection of David H. Yaghjian

Returning Home from the Grocery, 1945
Oil on board
15 x 21
Collection of Susan A. Yaghjian

Army Store, 1946
Oil on canvas
18 x 24
Collection of David Hodges

Assembly Street Market, 1946
Oil on board
20 x 30
Collection of Francis F. Hewitt

Night on Assembly Street, circa 1946
Oil on board
17 ¾ x 26
Collection of Candy Yaghjian Waites

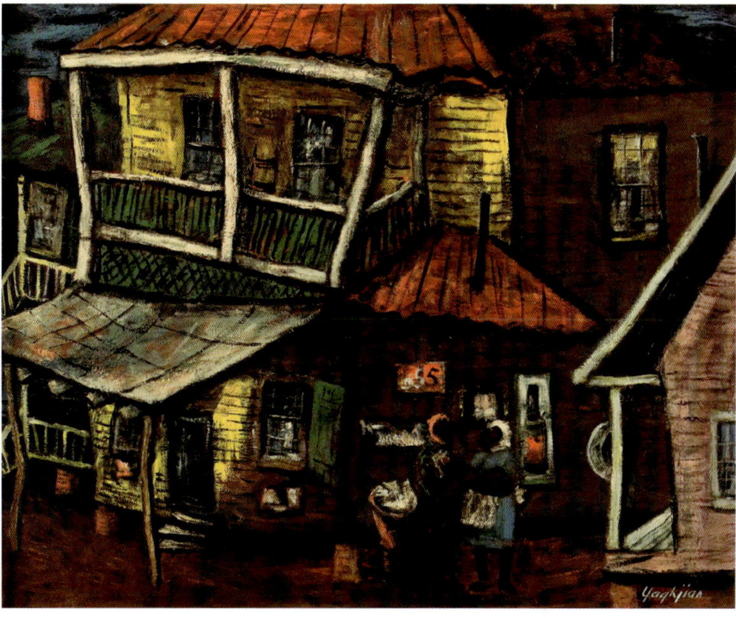

So I Said, circa 1955

Hopeville, circa 1948
Oil on canvas on board
16 x 20
Private Collection

Selling Her Vegetables, circa 1948
Oil on board
16 x 20
Collection of David H. Yaghjian

Back Stairs in Vermont, 1949
Oil on board
24 x 17
Collection of Candy Yaghjian Waites

Car Wrecks, 1949
Oil on cardboard
9 x 11
Collection of David H. Yaghjian

Kitchen in Wallingford, 1949
Oil on canvas
16 x 20
Collection of David H. Yaghjian

The Champ, 1949
Oil on canvas
27 ¼ x 31
On loan from Donald Kurtz

South Carolina Swamp, circa 1949
Oil on canvas
18 x 24
Collection of David H. Yaghjian

Snake Sketch, circa 1949
Graphite on paper
14 x 17
Private Collection

Drug Store on Corner at Night, circa 1950
Oil on canvas
14 x 20
On loan from the Steve and Darlene Coogler Collection, Greenville, SC

Around the Bend, circa 1950
Lacquer on board
20 x 28
On loan from the Johnson Collection

Water Tower #1, circa 1950
Ink on paper
13 ½ x 21 ½
Columbia Museum of Art

Passing the Time, circa 1950
Oil with acrylic on linen
16 x 20
Collection of the Bowie Art Center, Erskine College, Due West, SC

Olympia Water Tower, circa 1950
Pencil and crayon on paper
5 x 7
South Carolina State Museum Collection

Evening Service, circa 1950
Lacquer on board
16 x 20
Collection of Candy Yaghjian Waites

Huger Street Sketch, circa 1950
Graphite on paper
10 x 14
Collection of David Hodges

Columbia Fair, Hurry, Hurry, 1950
Oil on canvas
23 ½ x 32
Collection of David H. Yaghjian

Doorway Distraction, 1950
Oil on canvas
24 x 36
Collection of Candy Yaghjian Waites

Corner House for Sale, 1950
Oil on canvas
15 x 15
Collection of Candy Yaghjian Waites

At B Stables, 1950
Oil on canvas
16 x 26
Collection of David H. Yaghjian

Red Caboose, Yellow Sky, 1950
Oil on board
20 x 34
Collection of David H. Yaghjian

Assembly Street Market, circa 1950
Oil on board
20 x 30
Private Collection

The Gossips, circa 1950
Pencil and crayon on paper
5 x 7
Collection of David H. Yaghjian

Gervais Street Antique Shop, circa 1950
Oil on board
22 ½ x 28
Morris Museum of Art, Augusta, GA

College Street Living Room, 1951
Oil on canvas
20 x 26
Collection of Lisa Waites Austin

Living Room to Kitchen, 1951
Oil on canvas
12 x 16 ½
Collection of Candy Yaghjian Waites

Coal Car, 1953
Oil on board
21 ¾ x 28 ½
Columbia Museum of Art

Lower Floor of Barn, 1953
Lacquer on board
24 x 30
Collection of David H. Yaghjian

Lower Floor of Barn (Sketch), 1953
Ink on paper
13 ¾ x 17
Private Collection

Lower Floor of Barn (Sketch), 1953
Watercolor on paper
13 ¾ x 17
Private Collection

Charleston Scene, no date
Watercolor on paper
14 x 16 ½
Collection of the Bowie Art Center, Erskine College, Due West, SC

Morning on Huger Street, circa 1955
Lacquer on board
32 x 39 ½
Greenville County Museum of Art, purchase from the Arthur and Holly Magill Fund

Quarry Near Danby, circa 1955
Lacquer on board
19 x 26
Collection of David H. Yaghjian

Dumping on Wheat Street, circa 1955
Oil on board
21 x 31
Collection of Wade Cleveland

The Red Church, circa 1955
Oil on board
19 x 22 ½
From the collection of Mark B. Coplan, courtesy of Laura Coplan Scott and Richard W. Scott

So I Said, circa 1955
Lacquer on board
31 x 37
Columbia Museum of Art

Hay Barn, circa 1955
Lacquer on board
16 x 27 ½
Collection of David H. Yaghjian

Our Bedroom in Vermont, circa 1955
Oil on board
24 x 18
Collection of Candy Yaghjian Waites

White Gas Tanks, circa 1955
Lacquer on board
17 ¾ x 35 ¾
Collection of Wade Cleveland

Concrete Works, circa 1955
Lacquer on board
17 x 39
Collection of Tad and Maureen Mallory

Untitled (Sketch for State House from Senate Street), circa 1955
Watercolor on paper
15 x 19
Collection of John W. and Rita Bragg Cullum

Marble Quarry, 1956
Lacquer on board
29 x 35
Collection of David H. Yaghjian

Coal Yard, 1957
Lacquer on board
24 x 36
Collection of Carolina First

Pentecostal Holiness Church, circa 1960
Acrylic on canvas
29 x 35
Collection of Ted and Karen Ramsaur

Night by the Tracks, circa 1960
Lacquer on board
16 x 26
Collection of Candy Yaghjian Waites

The Hot Trumpet, 1964
Lacquer on board
35 x 24
Private Collection

Baker's Grocery, circa 1965
Oil on board with applied paper
23 ½ x 29 ¼
Collection of John and Marcie Baker

Bringing in Some Vegetables, circa 1965
Lacquer on board
18 x 40
On loan from the Johnson Collection

Want to Play Cops and Robbers?,
circa 1965
Lacquer on board
30 x 34
Collection of Candy Yaghjian Waites

Dave Brubeck, 1965
Polymer on board
36 x 24
Collection of Candy Yaghjian Waites

Master Cleaners, 1965
Lacquer on board
19 x 39.5
Courtesy of Clemson Advancement Foundation

Waiting for Business, circa 1965
Lacquer on board
36 x 48
Collection of David H. Yaghjian

Untitled [Antique Shop], 1966
Polymer on board
24 x 30
Estate of Jenny Clarkson Dreher

Shoppers on 5th Avenue, circa 1967
Acrylic on board
30 x 24
Collection of Sara Chastain

Orange Sky on Park Street, circa 1970
Acrylic on board
24 x 36
Collection of Candy Yaghjian Waites

Night at the Fair, 1970
Acrylic on board
30 x 36
South Carolina State Museum
Gift of Chuck Weldon

Upper Main at Night, 1970
Polymer on board
20 x 30
Private Collection

Barnwell Street Below Gervais, circa 1970
Acrylic on board
15 ½ x 20
Collection of David H. Yaghjian

All in a Row, 1971
Polymer on board
Size 14 ½ x 20
Collection of John W. and Rita Bragg Cullum

State House from Senate Street,
circa 1975
Polymer on board
24 x 30
Collection of Candy Yaghjian Waites

Old Barn in Danby, 1976
Acrylic on canvas
20 x 28
Collection Candy Yaghjian Waites

Park Street Grocery, circa 1975
Acrylic on Canvas
22 x 28
On loan from the Johnson Collection

Break from House Work, circa 1975
Acrylic on Board
15 x 24
On loan from the Steve and Darlene Coogler Collection, Greenville, SC

Works of art are listed as height by width and the size is measured in inches

Chronology

1905 Born February 16, Harpoot, Armenia *

1907 Immigrated to the United States, Providence, Rhode Island

1922 Graduated Providence High School

1926-1930 Rhode Island School of Design

1930-1932 Art Students League, New York

1932-1934 Taught privately in New York City

1934-1936 Taught Great Neck Preparatory School

1936-1938 Worked on Works Progress Administration and taught privately in New York City

1938-1942 Taught Art Students League

1941 Married Dorothy Candy

1941-1944 Taught Edgewood Park Junior College, New York

1943 Candy Yaghjian (Waites) born in New York City, New York

1944-1945 Guest Artist University of Missouri

1945 Robin Yaghjian (Hasslen) born in Columbia, Missouri

1945-1966 Professor and Head, Department of Fine Arts, University of South Carolina

1948 David Henry Yaghjian born in Columbia, South Carolina

1955 Susan Allison Yaghjian born in Columbia, South Carolina

1966-1972 Artist-in-Residence, University of South Carolina

1997 Died December 2

* previous publications have listed his birth year as 1903 or 1904. 1905 is based on records from Ellis Island.

Selected Exhibitions

1932
Nathaniel M. Vose Gallery, Providence, RI
Ten Younger Artists from New York, curated by Edmund Yaghjian. Following artists participated: Cecil Bell, Jan Bols, Burgoyne Diller, Dean Fausett, John W. Gregory, Will Goldberg, Chas. Trumbo Henry, John T. Robertson, Bernhard Schardt, and Edmund Yaghjian.

Grand Central Palace, New York, NY
Sixteenth Annual Exhibition of the Society of Independent Artists.

The American Art Association,
Spring Salon, Anderson Galleries, Salons of America, NY.

1933
Hotel Brevoort, New York, NY
New York Scenes.

Playhouse Gallery, One Man Show.

1934
Providence Art Club, Providence, RI
Fifty-fifth Annual Exhibition of Oil Paintings.

Arts Students League, New York, NY
Members Work.

Pennsylvania Academy of the Fine Arts, Philadelphia, PA
Annual Exhibition.

Annual Exhibition of the Providence Art Club
College Art Association traveling exhibition.

The Corcoran Gallery of Art, Washington, D.C.
National Exhibition of Art by the Public Works of Art Project.

National Academy of Design, New York, NY
One Hundred and Ninth Annual Exhibition.

1935
Kraushaar Gallery, New York, NY
Group exhibition.

Roerich Museum
International Art Center, New York, NY
Docks, Bridges and Waterways of New York by Contemporary Artists of the Metropolitan Area.

1936
The Fine Arts Gallery, New York, NY
Sixtieth Anniversary Exhibition of Members and Associates of the Art Students League.

Carnegie Institute, Pittsburgh, PA
International Exhibition of Paintings.

Whitney Museum, New York, NY
Third Biennial Exhibition of Contemporary American Painting.

1937
Pennsylvania Academy of Fine Arts, Philadelphia, PA
Thirty-second Annual Exhibition.

The Corcoran Gallery of Art, Washington, D.C.
Fifteenth Biennial Exhibition of Contemporary American Oil Paintings.

The Fine Arts Gallery, New York, NY
Annual Exhibition of Members and Associates of the Art Students League of New York.

1939
The Toledo Museum of Art, OH
Twenty-sixth Annual Exhibition of Selected Paintings by Contemporary American Artists.

New York World's Fair.

1940
Kraushaar Gallery, 730 Fifth Avenue, New York, NY
First One-Man Show, Nocturnal New York .

Rhode Island School of Design, Museum of Art,
Contemporary American Painting.

Providence Art Club, Providence, RI
Sixty-first Annual Exhibition of Paintings, Sculpture, Drawings and Prints

1941
Montclair Art Museum, Montclair, NJ
America Yesterday and Today.

Whitney Museum of American Art, New York, NY
Paintings by Artists Under Forty.

Oklahoma Art Center, WPA Art Program
Third Annual Competitive Exhibition of Lithography.

Federal Works Agency, Section of Fine Arts, Public Buildings Administration,
Exhibition of Watercolors for Decoration.

1942
Metropolitan Museum of Art, New York, NY
Artists for Victory, An exhibition of Contemporary American Art.

1943
The Art Students League of New York and The
American Fine Arts Society, New York, NY
Exhibition of Distinguished Artists.

1944
The Metropolitan Museum of Art, New York, NY
Portrait of America.

1945
Carnegie Institute, Department of Fine Arts
Portrait of America.

Carnegie Institute, Department of Fine Arts, Pittsburgh, PA
Paintings in the United States.

1946
The National Academy of Design, New York , NY
Third Annual Exhibition of Paintings of the Year
sponsored by Pepsi-Cola Company.

High Museum of Art, Atlanta, GA
Second Southeastern Annual Exhibition of Oils and Water Colors
Third Purchase Prize.

The National Academy of Design, New York , NY
Fourth Annual Exhibition, Paintings of the Year,
sponsored by Pepsi-Cola Company.

The Rochester Memorial Art Gallery, Rochester, NY
Fourth Annual Exhibition, Paintings of the Year,
sponsored by Pepsi-Cola Company.

1948
The Corcoran Gallery of Art, Washington, D.C.
Fourth Annual Exhibition, Paintings of the Year,
sponsored by the Pepsi-Cola Company.

The Toledo Museum of Art, Toledo, OH
Fourth Annual Exhibition, Paintings of the Year,
sponsored by the Pepsi-Cola Company.

1949
The Pennsylvania Academy of the Fine Arts, Philadelphia, PA
One Hundred and Forty-fourth Annual Exhibition of Painting and Sculpture.

1950
High Museum of Art, Atlanta, GA
Fifth Southeastern Annual Exhibition of Oils and Water
Colors by Artists of Eight Southeastern States.

1951
One-Man Exhibition at Columbia (SC) Museum of Art.

1953
The Metropolitan Museum of Art, New York, NY
American Water Colors, Drawings, and Prints,
A National Competitive Exhibition.

The High Museum of Art and The Scott Memorial Gallery, Atlanta, GA
Eighth Southeastern Annual Exhibition by
Artists of Eight Southeastern States.

Columbia Museum of Art, Columbia, SC
Carolina Five

1954
The Birmingham Museum of Art, Birmingham, AL
Steel, Iron and Man, A National Competition.

Norfolk Museum, Norfolk, VA
Exhibition of American Drawing Annual XII.

The Butler Institute of American Art, Youngstown, OH
Nineteenth Annual Midyear Show, An Exhibition of Oil and Water Color Paintings by Artists of the United States.

High Museum of Art, Atlanta, GA
Ninth Southeastern Annual Exhibition.

1955
Atlanta Art Association Galleries, Atlanta, GA
Tenth Southeastern Annual Exhibition by Artists of the Eight Southeastern States.

1958
The Guild of South Carolina Artists, Gibbes Art Gallery
Charleston, South Carolina Eighth Annual Exhibition.

The Butler Institute of American Art, Youngstown, OH
Twenty-third Annual Midyear Show, An Exhibition of Oil and Water Color Paintings by Artists of the United States.

The Atlanta Art Association Galleries, Atlanta, GA
Thirteenth Southeastern Annual Exhibition by Artists of Nine Southeastern States.

1959
The Chautauqua Art Association, Chautauqua, NY
Second National Jury Show.

The Atlanta Art Association Galleries, Atlanta, GA
Fourteenth Southeastern Annual Exhibition by Artists of Nine Southeastern States.

The Columbia Museum of Art, Columbia, SC
Second Columbia Painting Biennial, A Competition for Living American Artists.

1960
The George Thomas Hunter Gallery of Art, Chattanooga, TN
First Hunter Gallery Annual.

Gibbes Art Gallery, Carolina Art Association, Charleston, SC
Yaghjian 1945-1960.

1961
The Columbia Museum of Art, Columbia, SC
Investing in Art.

Sarasota Art Association, FL
Painting and Sculpture at the John and Mable Ringling Museum of Art.

The George Thomas Hunter Gallery of Art, Chattanooga, TN
Second Hunter Gallery Annual.

1965
Pittsburgh Plan for Art, Pittsburgh, PA

The Mint Museum, Charlotte, NC

The Winston Salem Gallery of Fine Art, Winston Salem, NC

The Madison Gallery, New York, NY

Galerie Fontainbleau, Miami Beach, FL

The Red Barn, Woodstock, VT

Gallery Two, Woodstock, VT

1966
The Ligoa Duncan Gallery, New York, NY
Edmund Yaghjian.

1967
Gallerie Internationale New York, NY
Edmund Yaghjian.

1972
Columbia Museum of Art, Columbia, SC
Edmund Yaghjian Retrospective Exhibition 1932-1972.

2007
South Carolina State Museum, Columbia, SC
Edmund Yaghjian: A Retrospective
March 16 – September 16

Selected Public Collections

Carolina First Collection

Columbia Museum of Art, Columbia, SC

Furman University, Greenville, SC

Gibbes Museum of Art, Charleston, SC

Greenville County Museum of Art, Greenville, SC

Morris Museum of Art, Augusta, GA

New York Public Library

New York University, Washington Square

Ossining Historical Society Museum, Ossining, NY

Smithsonian American Art Museum

South Carolina Arts Commission, State Art Collection, Columbia, SC

South Carolina State Museum, Columbia, SC

The Bowie Art Center, Erskine College, Due West, SC

The Clemson Advancement Foundation, Clemson, SC

West Point Museum, West Point, NY

Acknowledgements

In addition to the family of Edmund Yaghjian, and the collectors that have graciously loaned their paintings and drawings for the exhibition, the South Carolina State Museum would like to thank the following individuals for their support and help with this exhibition:

Archbishop Oshagan Choloyan

Ben Tanner, WIS TV Columbia

Beth Inman, Columbia Museum of Art

Bryan Jones, SC Department of Transportation

Claudia Beckwith, Greenville County Museum of Art

Heather Bacon, SC State Museum Art Intern

Jay Williams, Morris Museum of Art

Jodi Salter, Department of Art, University of South Carolina

Libby Coynor, Columbia Museum of Art

Martha Severens, Greenville County Museum of Art

Michael Hyder, SC State Museum Art Intern

Patricia Phagan, Vassar College

Sandra Rupp, Hampton III Gallery

Sara Myers, High Museum of Art

Todd Herman, Columbia Museum of Art

Virginia Mecklenburg, Smithsonian American Art Museum

Ashley Matheny

Irene Morrah

James Brannock

Lise Johnson

Sharon Brown